# 11+ Maths

## For **GL** Assessment

This CGP book is packed with 10-Minute Tests at just the right level for ages 9-10 — perfect for building up the skills they'll need for the GL 11+ tests.

What's more, we've included step-by-step answers for every question, plus a handy chart to keep track of their progress.  Everything you need!

## 10-Minute Tests

### Ages 9-10

---

### How to access your free Online Edition

This book includes a free Online Edition to read on your PC, Mac or tablet.
You'll just need to go to **cgpbooks.co.uk/extras** and enter this code:

## 3320 5885 3741 8295

By the way, this code only works for one person.  If somebody else has used this book before you, they might have already claimed the Online Edition.

# How to use this book

This book is made up of 10-minute tests and puzzle pages.
There are answers and detailed explanations at the back of the book.

## 10-Minute Tests

- There are 31 tests in this book, each containing 10 questions.

- Each test is designed to cover a good range of the question styles
  and topics that your child could come across in their 11+ test.

- Your child should aim to score at least 8 out of 10 in each 10-minute test.
  If they score less than this, use their results to work out the areas they need more practice on.

- If your child hasn't managed to finish the test in time, they need to work on increasing their
  speed, whereas if they have made a lot of mistakes, they need to work more carefully.

- Keep track of your child's scores using the progress chart on the inside back cover of the book.

## Puzzle Pages

- There are 12 puzzle pages in this book, which are a great break from test-style questions.
  They encourage children to practise the same skills that they will need in the test,
  but in a fun way.


Published by CGP

Editors:
Daniel Fielding, Emily Garrett, Rachael Rogers, Caroline Thomson

With thanks to Glenn Rogers for the proofreading.

Please note that CGP is not associated with GL Assessment in any way. This book
does not include any official questions and is not endorsed by GL Assessment.

ISBN: 978 1 78908 300 2
Printed by Zenith Print & Packaging Ltd, Pontypridd.
Clipart from Corel®

Based on the classic CGP style created by Richard Parsons.

# Contents


Test 1 ............................................ 2

Test 2 ............................................ 5

Test 3 ............................................ 8

**Puzzles 1** ........................................ **11**

Test 4 ............................................ 12

Test 5 ............................................ 15

**Puzzles 2** ........................................ **18**

Test 6 ............................................ 19

Test 7 ............................................ 22

Test 8 ............................................ 25

**Puzzles 3** ........................................ **28**

Test 9 ............................................ 29

Test 10 ........................................... 32

**Puzzles 4** ........................................ **35**

Test 11 ........................................... 36

Test 12 ........................................... 39

Test 13 ........................................... 42

**Puzzles 5** ........................................ **45**

Test 14 ........................................... 46

Test 15 ........................................... 49

**Puzzles 6** ........................................ **52**

Test 16 ........................................... 53

Test 17 ........................................... 56

Test 18 ........................................... 59

**Puzzles 7** ........................................ **62**

Test 19 ........................................... 63

Test 20 ........................................... 66

**Puzzles 8** ........................................ **69**

Test 21 ........................................... 70

Test 22 ........................................... 73

Test 23 ........................................... 76

**Puzzles 9** ........................................ **79**

Test 24 ........................................... 80

Test 25 ........................................... 83

**Puzzles 10** ....................................... **86**

Test 26 ........................................... 87

Test 27 ........................................... 90

Test 28 ........................................... 93

**Puzzles 11** ....................................... **96**

Test 29 ........................................... 97

Test 30 ........................................... 100

Test 31 ........................................... 103

**Puzzles 12** ....................................... **106**

Answers ........................................... 107

You have **10 minutes** to do this test.  Work as quickly and accurately as you can.

1. Aidan leaves his house at 8:15 am.  He arrives at work at 9:25 am
How long does his journey take?  Circle the correct answer.

> **A**    40 minutes
>
> **B**    50 minutes
>
> **C**    70 minutes
>
> **D**    80 minutes
>
> **E**    90 minutes

2. A sequence starts 3, 6, 12, 24, ...
What is the next term in the sequence?

Answer: ___________

3. Anne draws a diagram of her garden, shown below.

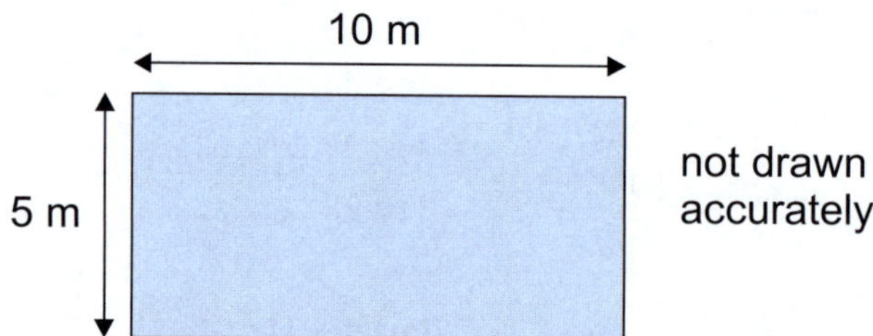


Anne wants to put a fence around the perimeter of her garden.
How many metres of fencing does Anne need to buy?

Answer: ___________ m

4.  Which of the following is not a prime number?
    Circle the correct option.

> **A**  19
>
> **B**  29
>
> **C**  39
>
> **D**  41
>
> **E**  61

5.  Nyala sees the following question in her homework.

> **Question:** What is $(54 - 42) \times 7$?

What is the correct answer?

Answer: _____________

6.  Laura has a bag of sweets.  This graph shows how many of each colour she has.

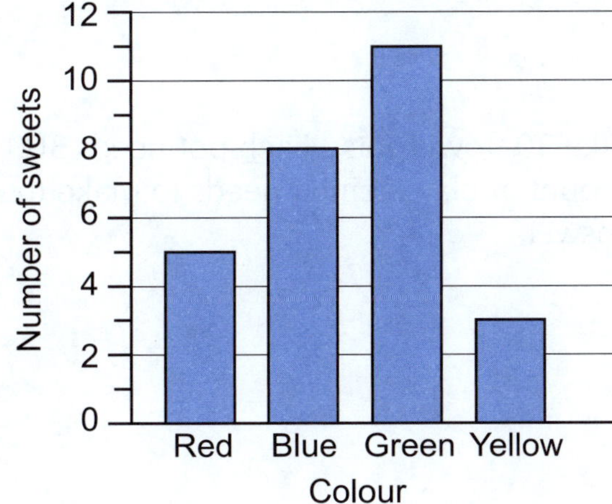


How many more green sweets than red sweets does she have?

Answer: _____________

7.  Which of the following is a common multiple of 4 and 5?
Circle the correct answer.

    **A**   30

    **B**   16

    **C**   25

    **D**   24

    **E**   40

8.  Samira walks 13.5 km on Saturday and 24.7 km on Sunday.
How far has she walked over the weekend, to the nearest kilometre?

Answer: __________ km

9.  Abdul has baked 20 cupcakes.  He gives 12 away to his friends,
then eats the rest.  What percentage of his cupcakes does Abdul eat?

Answer: __________ %

10. Jacinda wants to make 30 flowerpots.  Each pot needs 300 g of clay.
What is the total amount of clay Jacinda needs to make the flowerpots?
Circle the correct answer.

    **A**   90 000 g

    **B**   90 g

    **C**   9 kg

    **D**   0.9 kg

    **E**   1800 g

/ 10

⏱ **10**

You have **10 minutes** to do this test.  Work as quickly and accurately as you can.

1.  The table below shows Karin's best long jump distances on five different days.

| **Day** | Monday | Tuesday | Wednesday | Thursday | Friday |
|---|---|---|---|---|---|
| **Distance** | 3.5 m | 2.7 m | 3 m | 4.3 m | 4 m |

On which day did Karin jump the furthest?  Circle the correct answer.

**A**   Monday          **C**   Wednesday          **E**   Friday

**B**   Tuesday          **D**   Thursday

2.  In which of the following numbers does the 3 have the largest value?
Circle the correct option.

**A**   74 317.2

**B**   68 573

**C**   25 326

**D**   123 540

**E**   9178.3

3.  What is the size of angle $x$ in the triangle below?

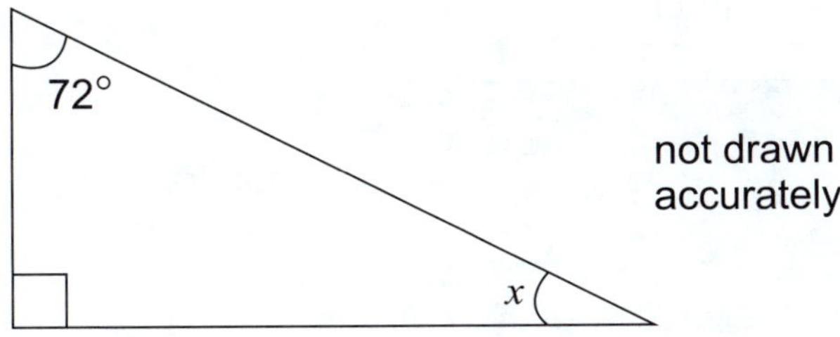


Answer: __________ °

4. On the grid below, point T is moved 5 squares left and 3 squares down.

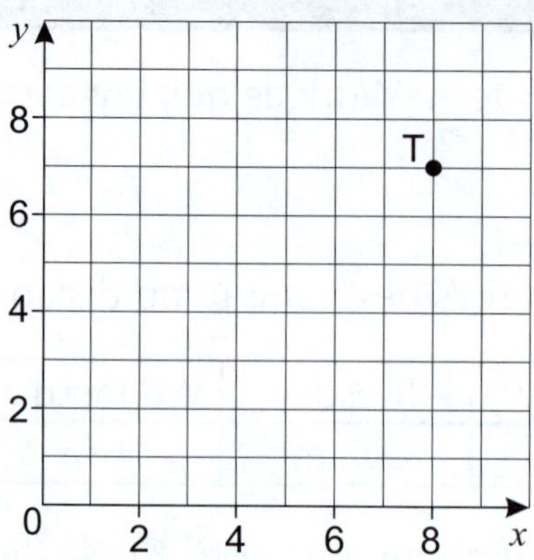

What are the new coordinates of point T?

Answer: ( ___________ , ___________ )

5. Billy goes to see a ballet. It starts at 7pm and is 1 hour and 40 minutes long, not including the interval. The interval happens halfway through the ballet and lasts for 25 minutes.

What time does the ballet finish?
Give your answer in 24-hour clock format.

Answer: ___________ : ___________

6. Work out the perimeter of the shape below.

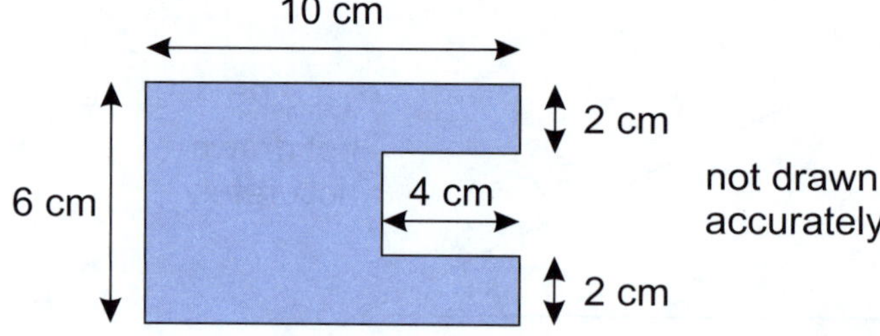


Answer: ___________ cm



6

7.  Which of the following is the biggest?  Circle the correct answer.

| | | | | | |
|---|---|---|---|---|---|
| **A** | $^3/_5$ | **C** | 33% | **E** | 6% |
| **B** | 0.25 | **D** | $^1/_{10}$ | | |

8.  Diego is making omelettes.  To make 3 omelettes he needs 6 eggs.
    If Diego wants to make 12 omelettes, how many eggs will he need?

Answer: ___________

9.  Nadine goes to visit a friend.  After 40 minutes in the car, she has completed
    50% of her journey.  How long does the journey to her friend's house take?
    Circle the correct answer.

    **A**   1 hour
    **B**   1 hour 10 minutes
    **C**   1 hour 20 minutes
    **D**   1 hour 30 minutes
    **E**   2 hours 10 minutes

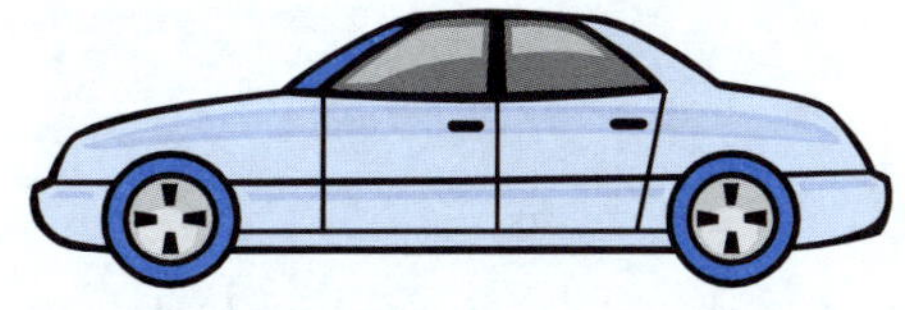

10.  Ed has 18 t-shirts.  Seven are red, six are blue and two are white.
     The rest of his t-shirts are green.  What fraction of Ed's t-shirts are green?
     Circle the correct answer.

| | | | | | |
|---|---|---|---|---|---|
| **A** | $^5/_6$ | **C** | $^3/_5$ | **E** | $^3/_7$ |
| **B** | $^1/_6$ | **D** | $^5/_{18}$ | | |

/ 10

# Test 3

You have **10 minutes** to do this test.  Work as quickly and accurately as you can.

1.  What is 56 782 rounded to the nearest hundred?

Answer: ____________

2.  This pictogram shows the number of ice creams Becky sells in one day.

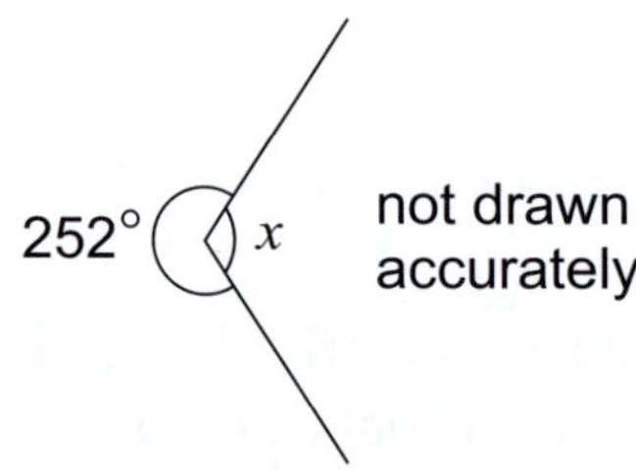



How many more vanilla ice creams than strawberry ice creams did Becky sell that day?

Answer: ____________

3.  What is the size of angle *x* below?



Answer: ____________ °

4.  A glass can hold 300 ml of water.
    How many whole glasses can be filled from a 2 litre jug of water?

Answer: ____________

5.  Sayeed has built this cuboid out of cardboard.

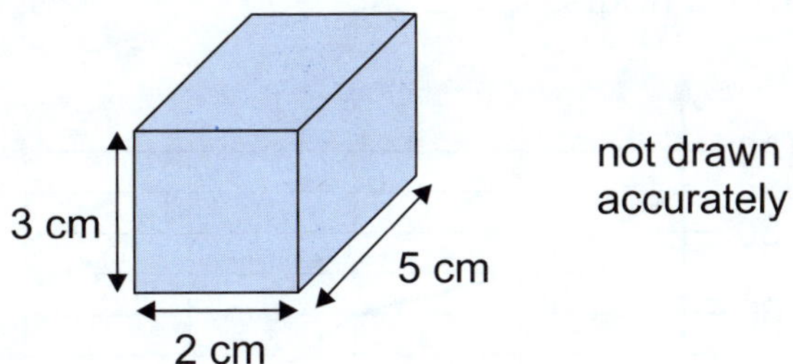



What is the volume of the cuboid?  Circle the correct option.

**A**  9 cm³        **C**  12 cm³        **E**  6 cm³

**B**  30 cm³       **D**  27 cm³


6.  The first five terms in a sequence are 2.5, 3.0, 3.5, 4.0, 4.5.
    What is the next number in the sequence?

Answer: ___________


7.  Martha draws a shape and a mirror line, shown below.

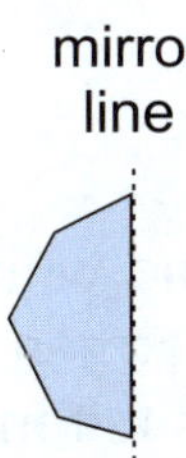



The shape and its reflection make a new shape.
What is the name of the new shape?  Circle the correct answer.

**A**    Rectangle          **C**    Hexagon          **E**    Octagon

**B**    Pentagon           **D**    Heptagon

8.  Ash draws a line graph to show how the temperature
    of a cup of tea falls over 2 hours.

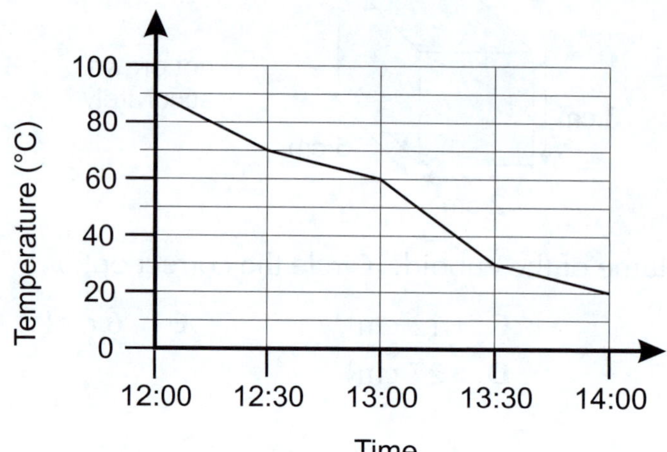


By how much did the temperature of Ash's tea decrease between 12:30 and 13:30?

Answer: __________ °C


9.  Which of these calculations gives an even number?  Circle the correct answer.

   **A**   5 + 9 + 7        **C**   3 + 11 + 11        **E**   23 + 25 + 21
   **B**   15 + 6 + 13      **D**   2 + 5 + 8


10. Carmen has a bag of black marbles and white marbles.  There are ten marbles in
    total, and seven of them are black.  Carmen removes one black marble from
    the bag.  What fraction of the marbles left in the bag are white?
    Circle the correct answer.

   **A**  $\frac{7}{9}$        **C**  $\frac{3}{10}$        **E**  $\frac{1}{3}$
   **B**  $\frac{6}{7}$        **D**  $\frac{2}{5}$

/ 10

Break time!  Have a crack at the **factor** and **number** puzzles below.

## The Postman's Factor Path

Percy the postman is delivering a letter to house number 12.
He can only walk in front of houses which have a factor of 24 on them.
Draw Percy's path on the map below.

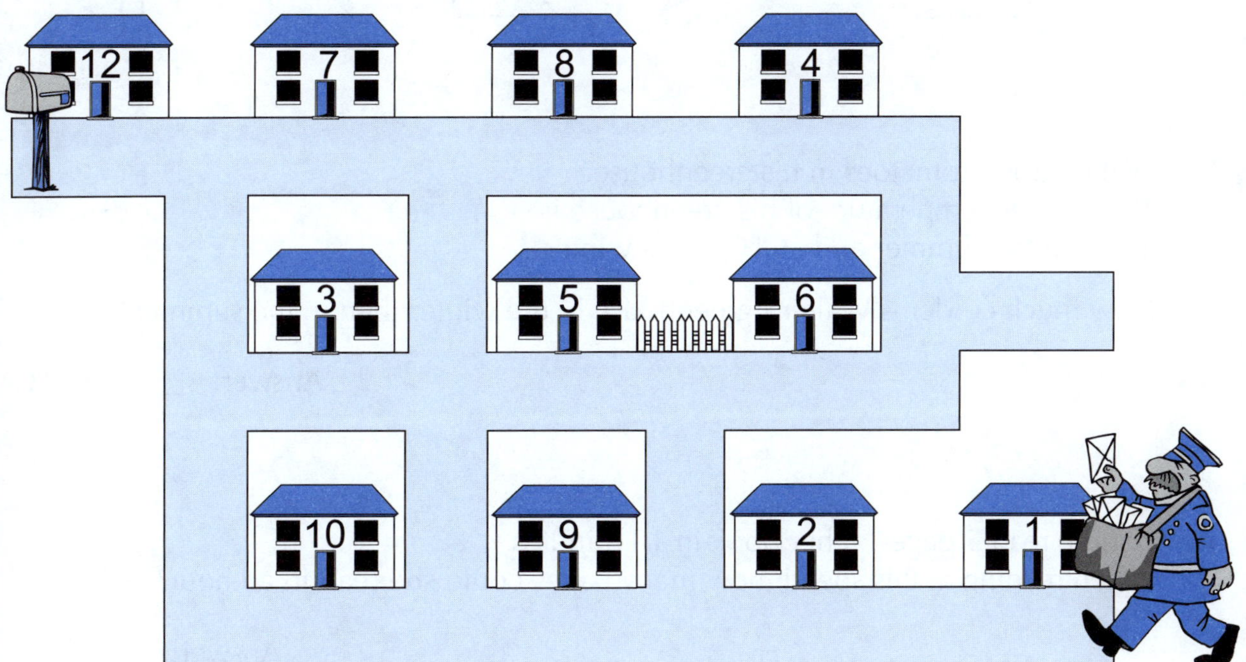


## Domino Dilemma

The Alverston Domino League has come to an end.
Unfortunately one player's score has gone missing:

56, 50, ?, 57, 54

Here are some clues to find out the missing score:

*"When the 5 scores are lined up in order of size, the middle one is 56."*
*"The difference between the highest score and the lowest score is 10."*

What is the missing score?

Answer: __________

You have **10 minutes** to do this test.  Work as quickly and accurately as you can.

1.    Which of these triangles has three acute angles?  Circle the correct option.

    A    B    C    D    E

2.    Walter grows tomatoes in his greenhouse.
    The average temperature of his greenhouse is
    20 °C in the summer and –6 °C in the winter.

    How much colder is Walter's greenhouse in the winter than in the summer?

    Answer: __________ °C

3.    Bonnie read 5 pages of her book in 10 minutes.
    When reading at this speed, how many pages could she read in an hour?

    Answer: __________

4.    Which of the following are both factors of 28?  Circle the correct option.

    A    2 and 3
    B    2 and 5
    C    2 and 7
    D    3 and 5
    E    3 and 7

5. The shape below is drawn on squared paper.  Each square has sides of 1 cm.
What is the area of the shape?

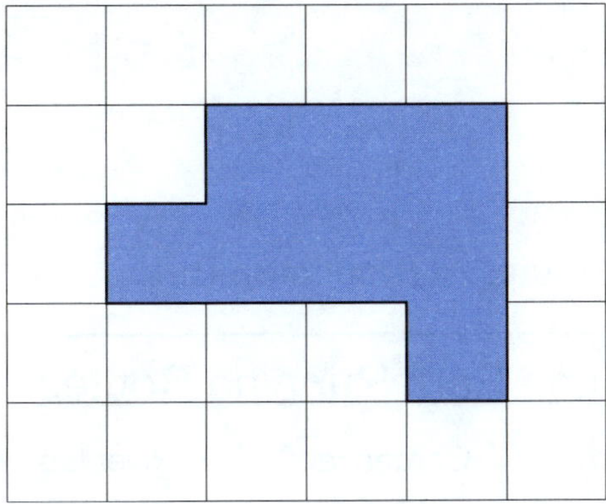

Answer: __________ cm²

6. What is 0.7 + 0.2 as a fraction?  Circle the correct option.

    **A** $^9/_{10}$          **C** $^1/_3$          **E** $^5/_6$

    **B** $^5/_{18}$         **D** $^1/_2$

7. Ali sells carrots and potatoes from her market stall.  Ali records how many carrots
and potatoes are sold each day.  She records her findings in the graph below.

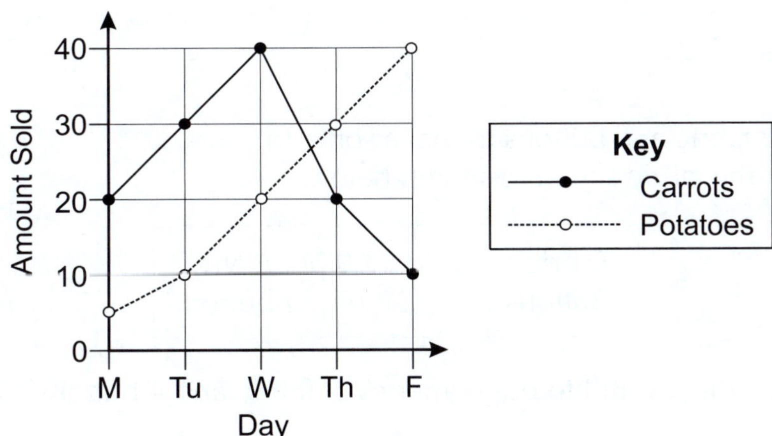


On which day did Ali start selling more potatoes than carrots?
Circle the correct option.

    **A** Monday        **C** Wednesday        **E** Friday

    **B** Tuesday        **D** Thursday

      13      Test 4

8.   A rectangle is 12 cm long.  Its width is 50% the size of its length.
     What is the perimeter of the rectangle?

Answer: __________ cm

9.   There are three running routes in Broughton Park.

### Broughton Park Running Routes

| Forest lap | Garden lap | River lap |
|------------|------------|-----------|
| 3 km | 0.5 km | 0.5 km |

Julia runs 3 forest laps and 5 garden laps.  How far does she run in total?
Circle the correct option.

  **A**   3.5 km
  **B**   15 km
  **C**   16.5 km
  **D**   8 km
  **E**   11.5 km

10.  Bill is buying fabric and buttons to make some trousers.
     The prices in the fabric shop are shown below.

| | |
|--------|------------------|
| Fabric | £5.60 per metre |
| Buttons | £1.10 per button |

How much will it cost Bill to buy 2 metres of fabric and 4 buttons?

Answer: £__________

/ 10

You have **10 minutes** to do this test.  Work as quickly and accurately as you can.

1.  Satoshi draws a shape on some squared paper.  Each square has an area of 1 cm².

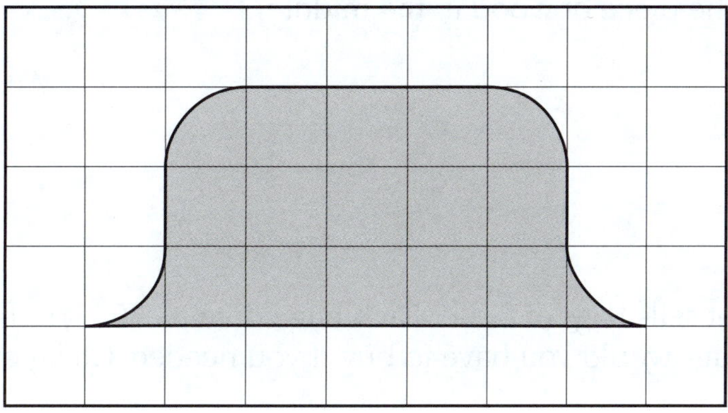

Estimate the area of the drawing.

Answer: __________ cm²

2.  The triangle below has two angles which are 50°.
    What is the size of the third angle?

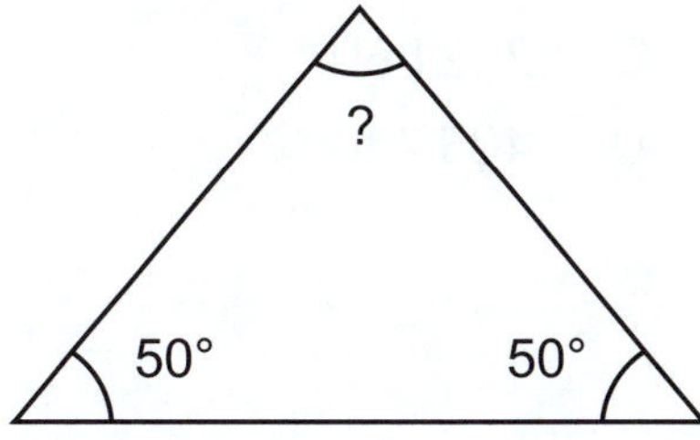


Answer: __________ °

3.  Mariposa owns two horses, three cows and five chickens.

    What fraction of all her animals are chickens?
    Circle the correct option.

    **A**  ³/₁₀        **C**  ²/₉        **E**  ⁵/₈
    **B**  ¹/₂         **D**  ¹/₇

4. Ishan is collecting firewood.  He collects wood of different lengths, as shown in the list below.

25 cm    19 cm    42 cm    30 cm    35 cm

Ishan lays his firewood on the floor, in order of length.
How long is the piece of wood in the middle?

Answer: _____________ cm

5. A supermarket sells bags of flour.  Each bag contains 500 g of flour.
How many bags would you have to buy if you needed 1.6 kg of flour?

Answer: _____________

6. | $4830 \times 21 = 101\,430$ |   What is $4830 \times 42$?  Circle the correct answer.

| | | |
|---|---|---|
| **A**  115 430 | **C**  202 860 | **E**  50 715 |
| **B**  193 200 | **D**  405 720 | |

7. A courier service completes 40 journeys from Willowdale to Birchbeck every year.
20% of those journeys arrive in Birchbeck late.

How many times does the courier service arrive late in Birchbeck each year?

Answer: _____________

8.  Marcus has ★ apps on his phone.  Marcus has 3 more apps than John.
    Which expression gives the number of apps John has on his phone?
    Circle the correct answer.

    **A**  ★ – 3        **C**  ★ + 3        **E**  3 – ★

    **B**  3★         **D**  ★ ÷ 3

9.  A building is 10 m tall.  A 350 cm extension is added to the top of the building.
    What is the new height of the building?  Write your answer in metres.

Answer: __________ m

10. A triangle is drawn on the grid below.  Point P is a point on the triangle.

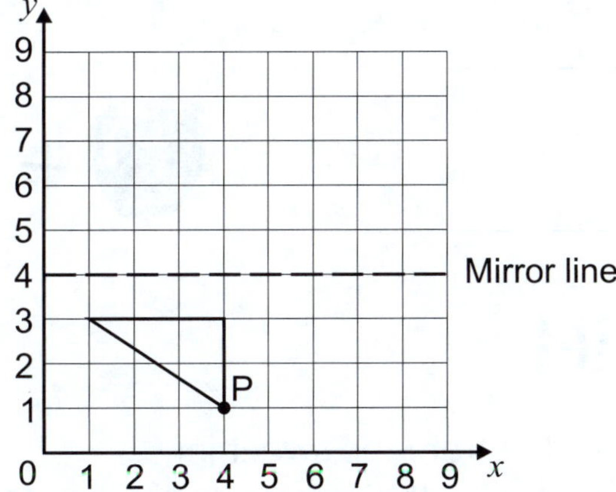


The triangle is reflected in the mirror line.
What are the coordinates of the reflection of point P?

Answer: ( __________ , __________ )

/ 10

Get stuck into these puzzles!  They're a great way to practise your **problem-solving** skills.

# Market Maths Mayhem

A market seller uses these three equations to work out how much she should charge for each item of food.  Use the information below to work out the missing values.

$$\text{bread} = 50p$$

$$\text{apple} = \underline{\hspace{3cm}}$$

$$\text{carrot} = \underline{\hspace{3cm}}$$

$$\text{tomato} = \underline{\hspace{3cm}}$$

$$\text{bread} - \text{apple} = 30p$$

$$\text{carrot} - \text{apple} = \text{apple}$$

$$\text{apple} + \text{carrot} = \text{tomato}$$

# The Sweet Thief

Some sweets have been stolen from the sweet jar.
Alfred, Bilal and Chichi each give their account of who stole the sweets.

Chichi <u>lies</u> by saying, *"Bilal is telling the truth."*

Bilal says, *"Alfred is telling the truth."*

Alfred says, *"I didn't steal the sweets!"*

Use the information above to find out who stole the sweets.

The person who stole the sweets is _______________________________________

You have **10 minutes** to do this test.  Work as quickly and accurately as you can.

1.    Harrison draws the following shapes.

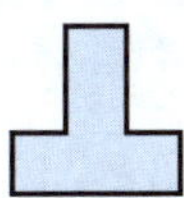 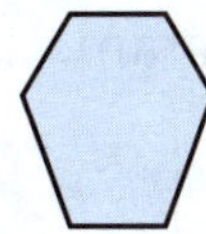  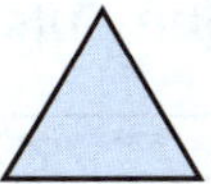 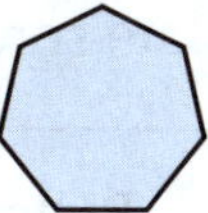

What fraction of these shapes are regular polygons?

Answer: __________

2.    Amjad buys chocolate bars for 10p each.  He sells them for 50p each.
      How much profit does he make by selling 15 chocolate bars?

Answer: £ __________

3.    Sharon makes handmade greetings cards.
      She records how many cards she makes each day in the table below.

| Mon | Tue | Wed | Thu | Fri | Sat | Sun |
|-----|-----|-----|-----|-----|-----|-----|
| 18  | 30  | 24  | 18  | 22  | 28  | 36  |

Which of the following statements is true?  Circle the correct option.

   **A**    Sharon made more cards on Tuesday than any other day.

   **B**    Sharon made 50 cards in total on Saturday and Sunday.

   **C**    Sharon made an even number of cards every day.

   **D**    Sharon made the fewest number of cards on Friday.

   **E**    Sharon made 14 more cards on Tuesday than on Thursday.

4.    The first four numbers in a sequence are: 19, 23, 27, 31.
      What will the fifth number in the sequence be?

Answer: ___________


5.    Chantelle asks her classmates whether they prefer toast with butter, jam,
      or chocolate spread.  She puts the results in a pictogram.

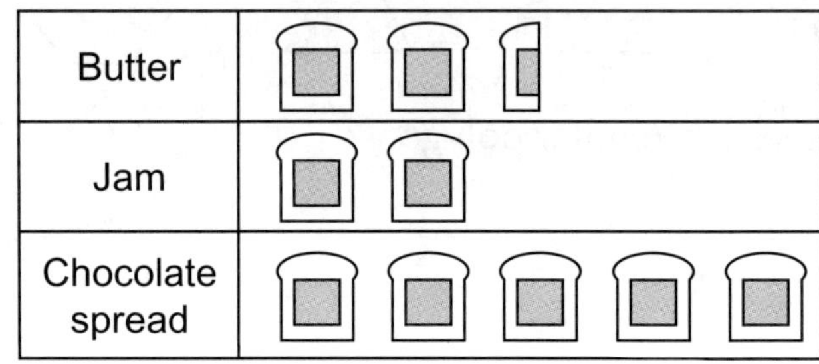


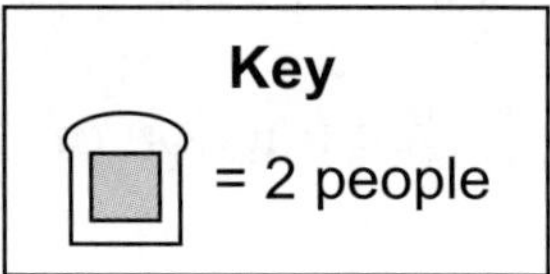


      How many more people said they prefer chocolate spread
      than butter on their toast?

Answer: ___________


6.    Richard sold 17 phone chargers during one week.
      Richard makes £5 on every phone charger he sells.
      How much money did he make on chargers during the week?

Answer: £ ___________


7.    Emily buys some vegetables.  She buys 4 carrots, 2 parsnips,
      3 onions and 1 potato.  What percentage of the vegetables are carrots?
      Circle the correct answer.

      **A**   40%            **C**   10%            **E**   5%
      **B**   20%            **D**   1%

8.   Leeroy turns half a turn clockwise, then another 90° clockwise.
     How many degrees has he turned in total?  Circle the correct answer.

     **A**   360°

     **B**   −45°

     **C**   180°

     **D**   270°

     **E**   135°

9.   This diagram shows a mirror with an area of 66 cm².

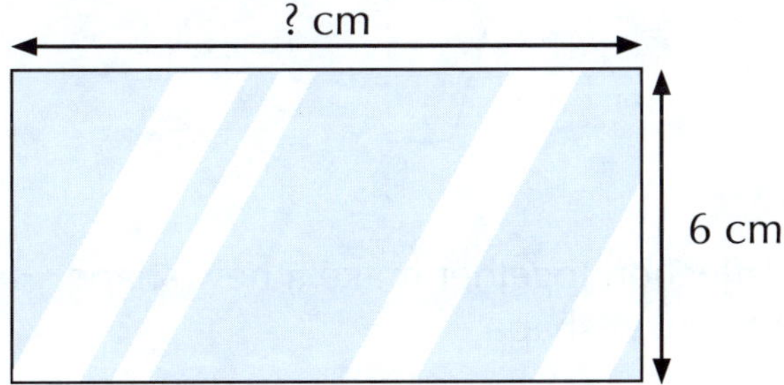



How long is the missing side of the mirror?

Answer: __________ cm

10.  Clive and Jenny are sharing a 600 ml bottle of orange juice.
     Clive drinks $^1/_4$ of the juice, then Jenny drinks $^1/_2$ of the remaining juice.
     How much orange juice is left?

Answer: __________ ml

/ 10

You have **10 minutes** to do this test.  Work as quickly and accurately as you can.

1.  A takeaway box of scampi holds 6 pieces.
    How many boxes should Tuscany buy if she wants 20 pieces of scampi?

    Answer: __________

2.  This shape is reflected in the dotted mirror line.

    The shape and its reflection together make a new shape.
    Circle the name of the new shape.

    **A**  Pentagon        **C**  Octagon        **E**  Quadrilateral

    **B**  Hexagon         **D**  Heptagon

3.  A triangle has been drawn on the coordinate grid, as shown below.

    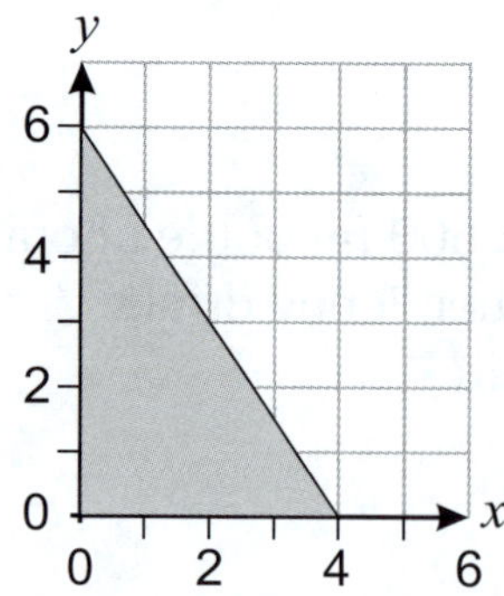

    Which of these points is inside the triangle?  Circle the correct answer.

    **A**  (1, 5)        **C**  (2, 5)        **E**  (3, 5)

    **B**  (1, 4)        **D**  (2, 4)

    22    

4.  Cole is comparing his Year 4 and Year 5 test results.

|        | Maths | English | Science |
|--------|-------|---------|---------|
| Year 4 | 20    | 10      | 25      |
| Year 5 | 25    | 15      | 25      |

Cole's total score for each year is calculated by adding his test results for Maths, English and Science.  What was his total score for Year 5?

Answer: __________

5.  Mr Jermy makes a scarecrow from 3 bales of straw,
2 pieces of cloth and 1 piece of wood.
He spends £12.75 on straw.  How much is a bale of straw?

Answer: £ __________

6.  Aishwarya takes part in a 10 km run once a month.
Last month it took her 60 minutes to complete the run.
This month, her time to complete the run was 10% lower.

How long did it take Aishwarya to complete the 10 km run this month?

Answer: __________ minutes

7.  Dean has two boxes that contain 20 toys each, and three boxes that contain 10 toys each.  What square number is closest to the total number of toys Dean has?

Answer: __________

8.   Which of these would you most expect to weigh 10 000 kg?
     Circle the correct answer.

     **A**   A pencil
     **B**   A bus
     **C**   A computer
     **D**   A dog
     **E**   A tiger


9.   The first five terms in a sequence are shown below.

     | ? | | 17 | | 24 | | 31 | | 38 |

     What number is the '?' in this sequence?

     Answer: ___________


10.  Tessa is playing a game.  She slides black stones towards a target area.
     Each ring shows the number of points she gets if a black stone stops in it.

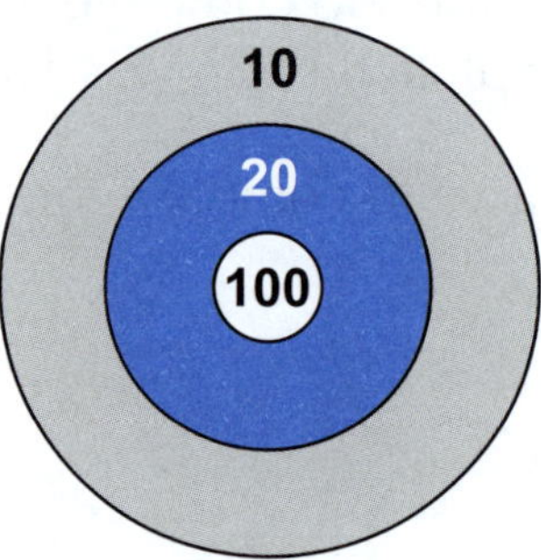


     What is the fewest number of stones needed to get exactly 290 points in total?

     Answer: __________

/ 10

You have **10 minutes** to do this test.  Work as quickly and accurately as you can.

1. The diagram shows a cuboid made out of 1 cm³ blocks.

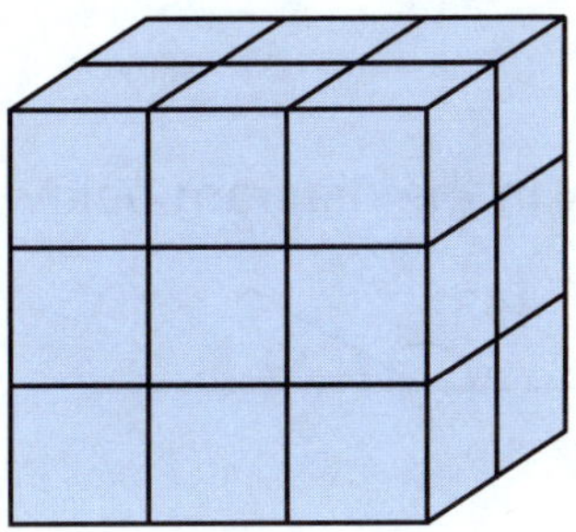

   What is the volume of this cuboid?

   Answer: ___________ cm³

2. Circle the most suitable unit for measuring the length of a car.

   **A**   km
   **B**   cm
   **C**   m
   **D**   m²
   **E**   kg

3. A regular pentagon has sides of length 12 cm.
   What is the perimeter of the pentagon?

   Answer: ___________ cm

4.  Sarah sets off from home and walks for 1 hour and 20 minutes.
    It takes her 50 minutes to jog back home.  How long does her whole journey take?
    Circle the correct answer.

    **A**   2 hours 30 minutes      **C**   30 minutes      **E**   3 hours

    **B**   150 minutes      **D**   130 minutes

5.  What is the size of the angle $x$ in the diagram below?

Answer: __________ °

6.  This graph shows how the price of a video game changes over 6 months.

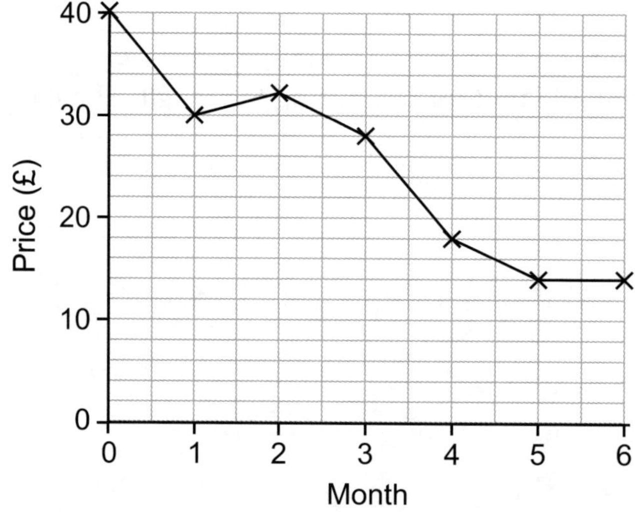


What is the difference in the price of the video game between
the start of month 2 and month 6?

Answer: £ __________

7.  Charlie has written down the following problem.

$$\heartsuit \div \blacktriangle = 4 + 5$$

If $\blacktriangle = 3$, what does $\heartsuit$ equal?

Answer: ___________


8.  What is 678.45 rounded to the nearest tenth?  Circle the correct answer.

**A**  678          **B**  678.5          **C**  678.4          **D**  680          **E**  679


9.  Write the following Roman numeral in numbers.

**XCIV**

Answer: ___________


10.  Gerald and Hashim have a total of 11 pencils between them.
Circle the letter of the statement that could be true.

**A**    Gerald and Hashim have 6 or more pencils each.
**B**    Gerald and Hashim have the same number of pencils.
**C**    Gerald and Hashim both have an even number of pencils.
**D**    Gerald has 3 pencils and Hashim has three times as many as Gerald.
**E**    Hashim owns 3 pencils more than Gerald.

/ 10

These puzzles are all about **multiplication** and **number sequences**.  Jump right in!

# Primes and Ca-nines

Bill and Ben are twins.  They are both going to a dentist who wants to remove all of their teeth which have either a:

> multiple of 9
>
> prime number greater than 9

Who will have the fewest teeth left? __________

How many fewer teeth will they have than their twin? __________

# Where Goes the Hare?

A hare starts on platform 1 and jumps in a sequence along each platform, following the arrows.

**Sequence 1:**
The hare jumps forward one platform, then two platforms, then three platforms.  He stops for a rest.

What number platform does he rest on? __________

He goes back to platform 1, then tries sequence 2.

**Sequence 2:**
The hare jumps forward 3 platforms, then jumps backward 1 platform.  He does this four more times, before stopping to eat a carrot.

What number platform does he eat his carrot on? __________

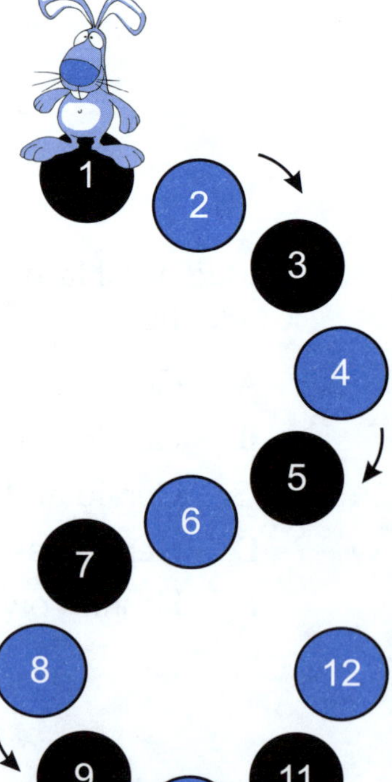

You have **10 minutes** to do this test.  Work as quickly and accurately as you can.

1.  The timetable below shows the times that a train stops at four different stations.

| Hopford | Jumpville | Skipmouth | Leapfield |
|---------|-----------|-----------|-----------|
| 07:00   | 07:55     | 09:10     | 09:55     |

Dennis gets on the train at one station.  1 hour and 15 minutes later, he gets off the train at another station.  Between which two stations did he travel?  Circle the correct answer.

    **A**    Hopford and Jumpville.

    **B**    Hopford and Skipmouth.

    **C**    Jumpville and Skipmouth.

    **D**    Jumpville and Leapfield.

    **E**    Hopford and Leapfield.

2.  Look at the diagram below.

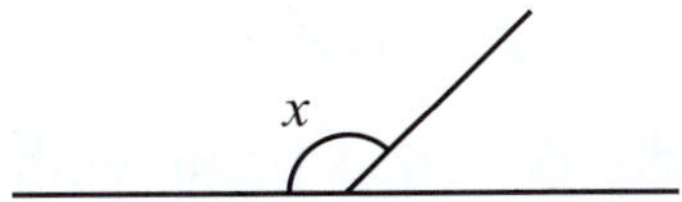


Circle the best estimate for the size of angle $x$ from the options below.

    **A**  60°      **B**  300°      **C**  90°      **D**  135°      **E**  45°

3.  An earthworm grows 0.02 m each year.
    How many years will it take to grow from 2 cm to 8 cm?

Answer: _____________ years

4.    Lishan is making 3D shapes using 1 cm³ blocks.

What is the total volume of Lishan's 3D shape?

Answer: _____________ cm³

5.    30 children record the first letter of their name.
The results are shown on the graph below.

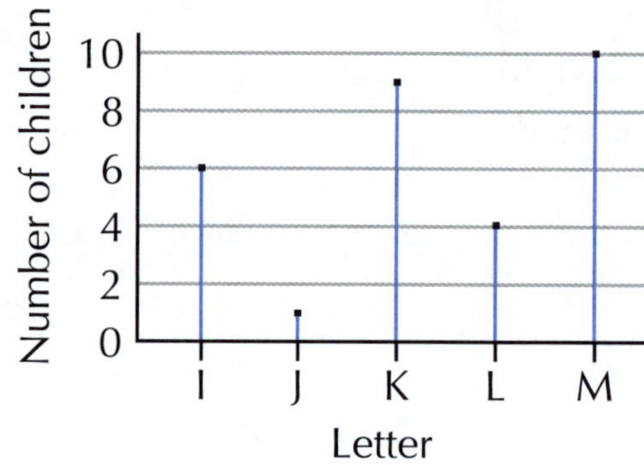


What fraction of all the children's names begin with the letter J?
Circle the correct option.

A   $\frac{1}{2}$        B   $\frac{1}{15}$        C   $\frac{1}{30}$        D   $\frac{2}{3}$        E   $\frac{2}{5}$

6.    What is 1352 to the nearest 100?

Answer: _____________

            

7.  What is the largest number in Roman numerals that can be made using all
    three cards below?

| V | X | I |

Answer: ___________


8.  The first three terms in a sequence of triangles are shown below.

    How many triangles will there be in the next term of the sequence?

Answer: ___________


9.  Doris is making gingerbread men for her 9 grandchildren.
    90 g of flour makes enough gingerbread men for 3 of her grandchildren.

    How much flour does she need to make enough gingerbread men for
    all of her 9 grandchildren?

Answer: ___________ g


10. Beatrice measures the temperature in her attic.
    At 8 am the temperature is 8 °C.
    If the temperature of her attic rises by 2 °C every hour,
    how many hours will it take until the attic reaches 18 °C?

Answer: ___________ hours

/ 10

You have **10 minutes** to do this test.  Work as quickly and accurately as you can.

1.   An equilateral triangle has a side of length 4 cm.  What is its perimeter?

Answer: ___________ cm

2.   A quail egg is placed on some weighing scales.

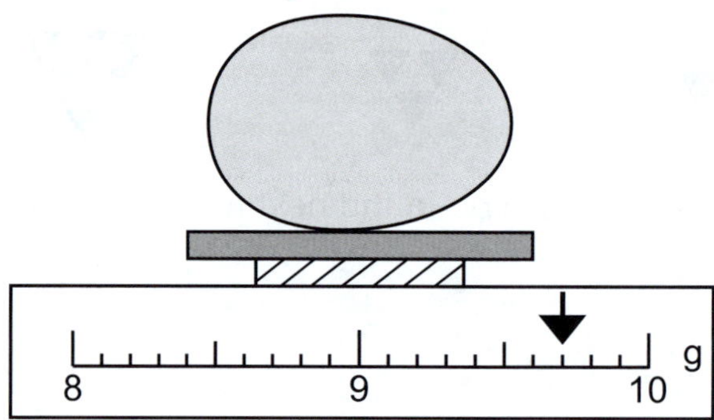


How much does the quail egg weigh?

Answer: __________ g

3.   Hakim goes to the zoo.  A zookeeper tells Hakim that one of the emperor penguins is 115 cm tall.  The zookeeper then tells him that one of the giraffes is 4 times taller than the emperor penguin.

How tall is the giraffe?  Give your answer in metres.

Answer: __________ m

4.   A bag contains sweets that are either blue, green or yellow.
$^1/_7$ of the sweets are blue and $^2/_7$ are green.
What fraction of the sweets are yellow?  Circle the correct answer.

   **A** $^1/_7$        **B** $^2/_7$        **C** $^3/_7$        **D** $^4/_7$        **E** $^5/_7$

5.    Rhiannon is describing a shape.  She says, "My shape has three sides and none of the angles are equal."  What shape is she describing?  Circle the correct answer.

   **A**    Equilateral triangle

   **B**    Quadrilateral

   **C**    Scalene triangle

   **D**    Pentagon

   **E**    Isosceles triangle

6.    Sebastian carries out a survey.  He asks a group of people how many hours they spend exercising each day.  The bar chart shows the results.

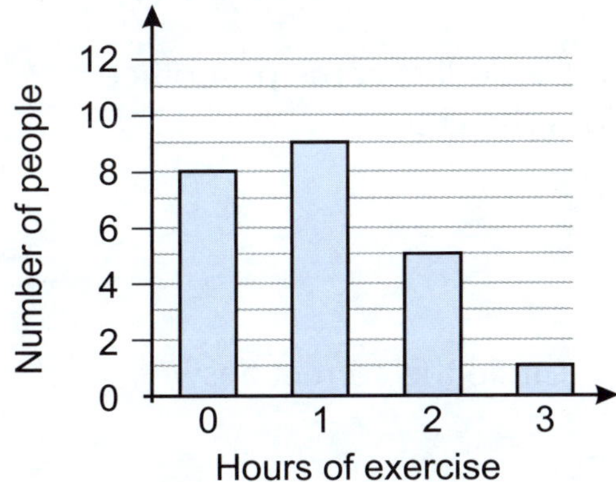


How many people said they exercised for 2 or more hours?

Answer: __________

7.    It costs £12.50 to hire a black suit for an hour and £50 to hire a white suit for a whole day.

How much cheaper would it be to hire a white suit for a whole day than a black suit for 7 hours?

Answer: £ __________

8.  The graph below shows the exchange rate between US dollars ($)
    and GB pounds (£) at a local post office.

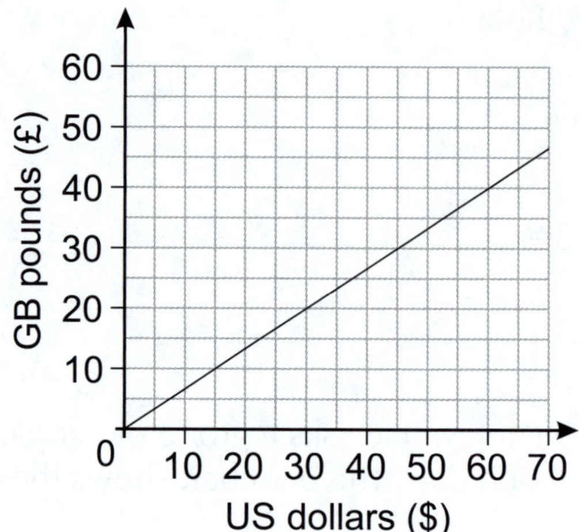

    Ola changes £20 into US dollars at the post office.
    How many dollars does she get?

    Answer: $ ______________


9.  What is $^4/_5 - ^1/_5 + ^3/_5$?  Circle the correct answer.

    **A**   $^7/_5$
    **B**   0
    **C**   $1^1/_5$
    **D**   $1^2/_5$
    **E**   $-1^1/_5$


10. If ⬠ = 5, ⬡ = 6 and ◯ = 10, what does the calculation below equal?

    (⬠ + ⬡) × ◯

    Answer: ______________


/ 10

Try out these puzzles to practise your knowledge of **numbers** and **symmetry**.

## Parcel Panic

Jerry is angry because the delivery service has sent him the wrong box.

Jerry describes the box that he was expecting:

*"My box has a number that is lower than half the number on this box."*

*"The number on my box is a multiple of 3."*

*"The number on my box is 1 less than a prime number."*

Which of the following is Jerry's box?  Circle the correct answer.

## Bizarre Biscuits

Stacy has made some oddly shaped biscuits.
The shapes of the biscuits are shaded on the grids below.

Draw one line on each shape to split it into two identical smaller biscuits.

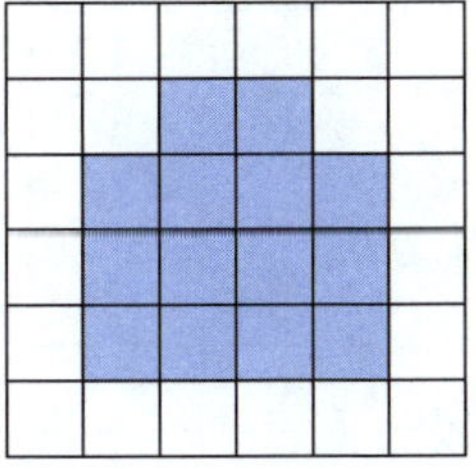
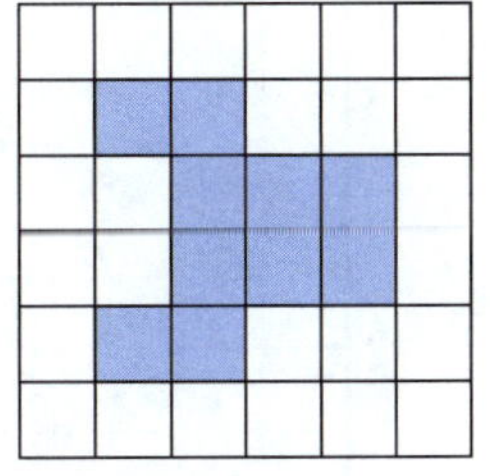
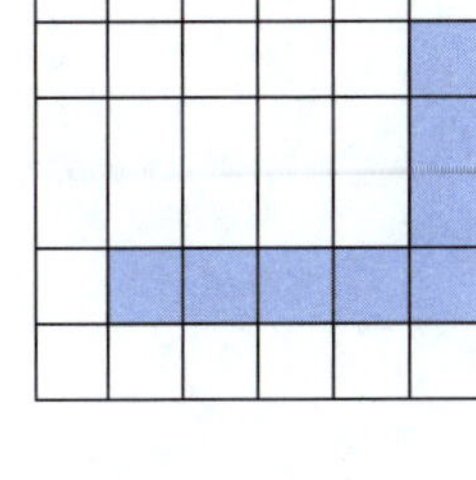

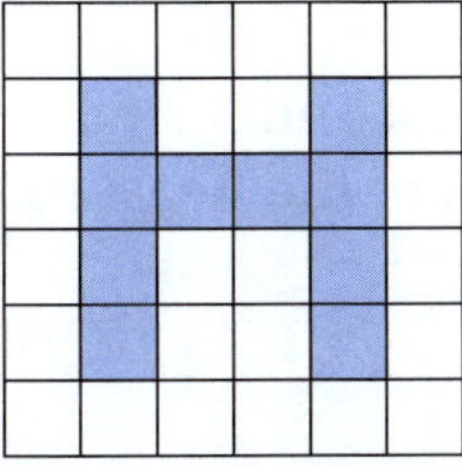

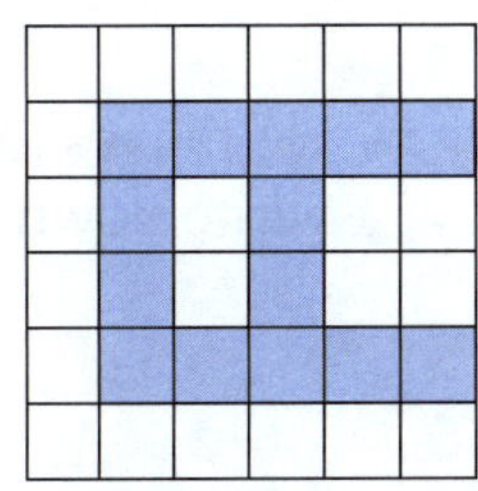

You have **10 minutes** to do this test.  Work as quickly and accurately as you can.

1.   What number is the arrow pointing to on this number line?

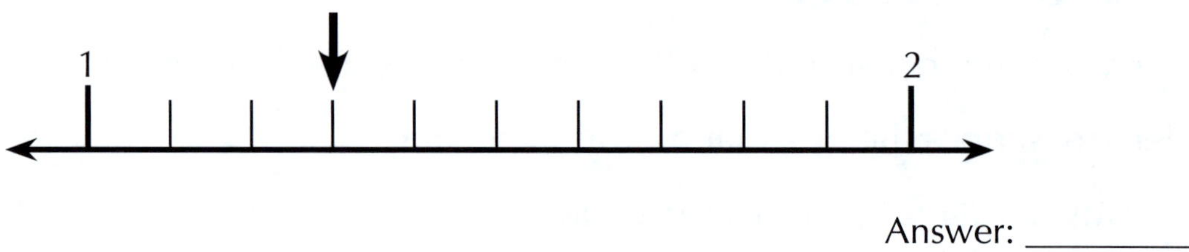

Answer: ___________

2.   What type of angle is shown below?  Circle the correct answer.

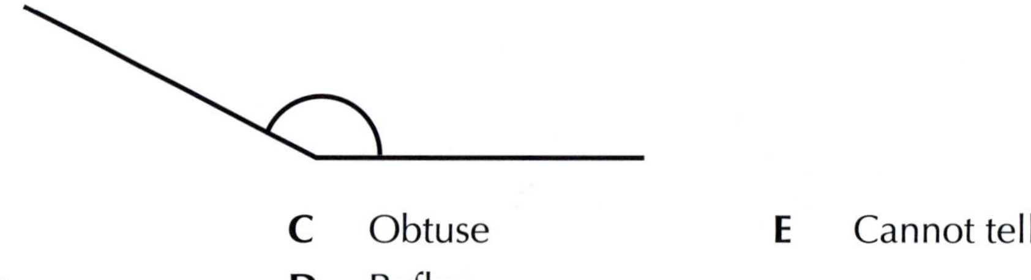

| | | |
|---|---|---|
| **A**   Acute | **C**   Obtuse | **E**   Cannot tell |
| **B**   Right angle | **D**   Reflex | |

3.   Lukas finds some treasure buried at the cross (×) on the map below.

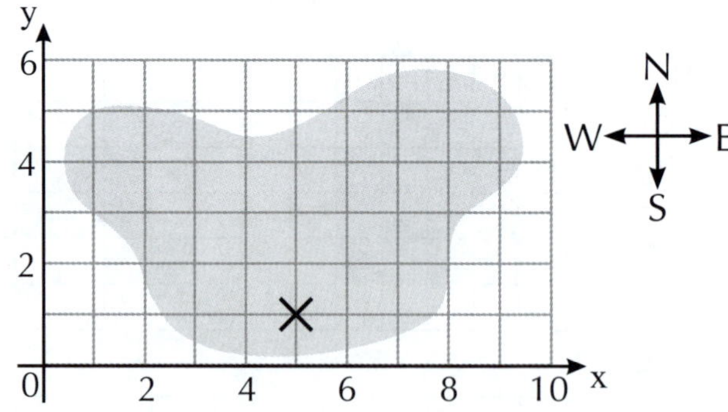


He moves the treasure 4 squares east and 3 squares north of where it was found.
Write down the coordinates of where the treasure is moved to.

Answer: ( ___________ , ___________ )

4.    Which of these shapes has only one line of symmetry?  Circle the correct option.

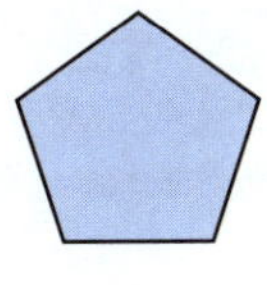 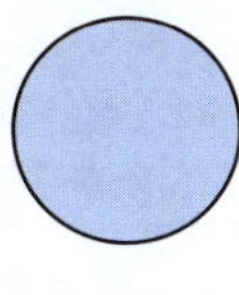 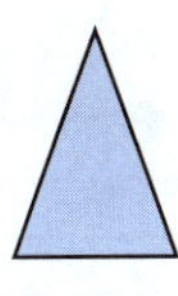 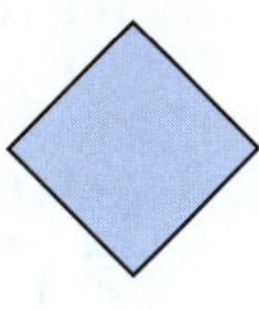 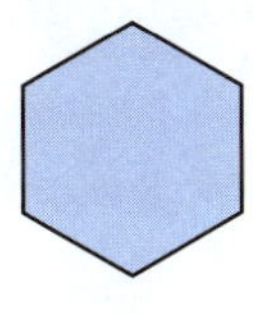

**A**            **B**            **C**            **D**            **E**

5.    Ravi weighs his five rabbits, and lists their weights below.
      Circle the weight of his heaviest rabbit.

    **A**    1.8 kg        **C**    1.96 kg        **E**    1235 g

    **B**    1820 g        **D**    1974 g

6.    Zola draws this diagram of her garden.  Her pond is shown by the shaded area.
      Each square on her diagram is 1 m$^2$.

What is the area of Zola's pond?

Answer: __________ m$^2$

7.    Yelena has a book about mythical creatures.  She writes down how many pages are
      about different creatures in the table below.

| Creature | Number of pages |
|---|---|
| Unicorns | 35 |
| Dragons | 30 |
| Mermaids | 15 |
| Fairies | 20 |

What fraction of the pages are about dragons?  Circle the correct answer.

    **A**    $^1/_{10}$        **C**    $^3/_{10}$        **E**    $^3/_5$

    **B**    $^2/_4$        **D**    $^1/_5$

8.  Atis asks 32 of his friends what their favourite season is.
    This bar graph shows his results.

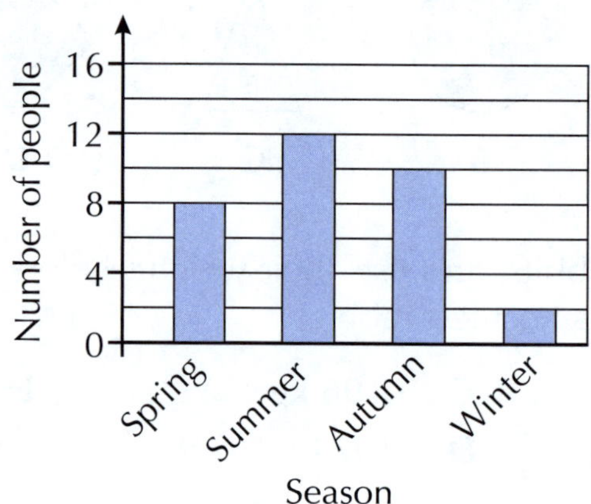

How many more people prefer summer to winter?

Answer: ___________

9.  Basil buys one apple (A) and one banana (B) for his lunch, three times a week.
    Which expression tells you how many apples and bananas he buys each week?
    Circle the correct option.

    **A**    $3A + B$
    **B**    $3A \times 3B$
    **C**    $A + B$
    **D**    $A + 3B$
    **E**    $3 \times (A + B)$

10. A tub of hummus costs £1.50, and a bag of carrot sticks costs 99p.
    Sabina buys three tubs of hummus and two bags of carrot sticks.
    How much does she spend in total?

Answer: £ ___________

/ 10

          

**10**

You have **10 minutes** to do this test.  Work as quickly and accurately as you can.

1.  Liam measured the heights of five people in his class.  His results are shown below.

| **Name** | Chloe | Duncan | Hannah | Jaspreet | Amit |
|---|---|---|---|---|---|
| **Height** | 1.23 m | 1.34 m | 1.47 m | 1.38 m | 1.5 m |

Out of the five people that Liam measured, who is the shortest?
Circle the correct answer.

**A**   Chloe

**B**   Duncan

**C**   Hannah

**D**   Jaspreet

**E**   Amit

2.  Vic divides 2000 g of lasagne into containers.
Each container can hold 300 g of lasagne.
What is the fewest number of containers she will need to store all the lasagne?

Answer: __________

3.  Grace pays £2.66 for 53 g of nutmeg.
How much would it cost Grace to buy 5300 g of nutmeg?
Circle the correct answer.

**A**   £26.60

**B**   £266.00

**C**   £200.66

**D**   £20.66

**E**   £260.60

4.   A DVD box set costs £12.  Each box set contains 6 DVDs.  Rose has £50.
     If she only buys box sets, what is the greatest number of DVDs she can get?

Answer: __________

5.   Richard is making jam.  His first jam jar can hold 400 g of jam.
     His second jar can hold 10% more jam than the first.
     How much jam can the second jar hold?  Circle the correct answer.

**A**   360 g

**B**   410 g

**C**   440 g

**D**   480 g

**E**   500 g

6.   This pictogram shows the number of hats sold by a hat shop at the weekend.

| Top hat | 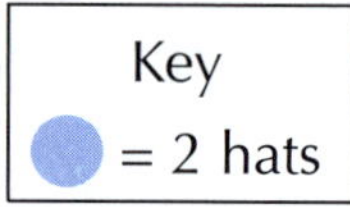 |
|---|---|
| Baseball cap | ●●● |
| Bobble hat | ●●●●● |

| Key |
|---|
| ● = 2 hats |

What fraction of all the hats sold at the weekend were baseball caps?
Circle the correct option.

**A**   $\frac{1}{6}$

**B**   $\frac{6}{19}$

**C**   $\frac{1}{3}$

**D**   $\frac{11}{19}$

**E**   $\frac{3}{10}$

7.  Chris leaves his house at 16:30 and drives to see his grandparents.
His journey takes 173 minutes.  What time does he get there?
Give your answer in the 24-hour clock format.

Answer: __________ : __________

8.  What is the volume of this cube?

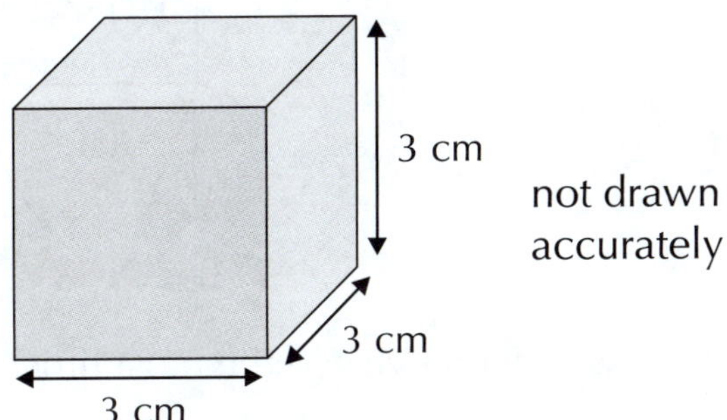


Answer: __________ cm³

9.  The first three patterns in a sequence are shown below.
How many circles will there be in the fifth pattern?

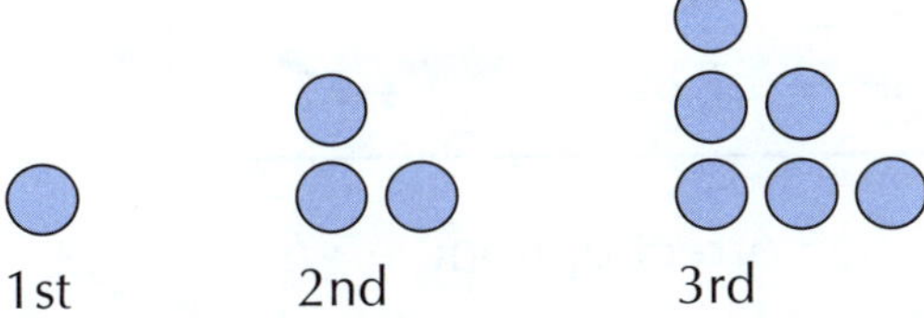


Answer: __________

10. Freya has an octagon-shaped rug.  Each side is 2.2 m long.
What is the perimeter of her rug?

Answer: __________ m

/ 10

You have **10 minutes** to do this test.  Work as quickly and accurately as you can.

1.  Amanda draws a pie chart to show the number of times she has visited 4 countries.

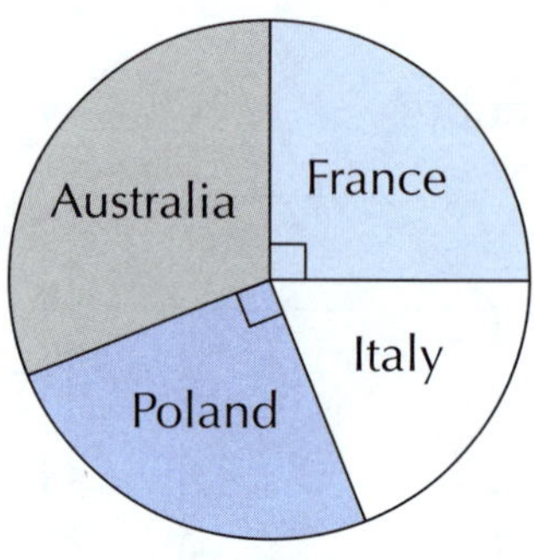


Which country has Amanda visited the most times?  Circle the correct option.

| | | | | | |
|---|---|---|---|---|---|
| **A** | Australia | **C** | Italy | **E** | Cannot tell |
| **B** | Poland | **D** | France | | |

2.  Shaun owns a local cafe.  The menu is shown below.

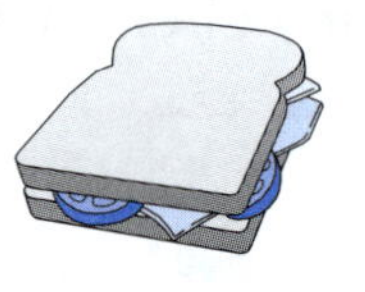

Soup — £1.60    Stew — £3.60
Sandwich — £3.20    Salad — £2.79
Cake — £2.95    Pork Pie — £1.80

Which of these statements is false?  Circle the correct option.

**A**  The most expensive item on the menu is the stew.

**B**  Soup is half the price of a sandwich.

**C**  Two soups cost less than £5.

**D**  A cake costs 26p more than a salad.

**E**  Stew costs 40p more than a sandwich.

3.  75 people are going on a trip to the zoo by minibus.
    Each minibus can carry 9 people.  How many minibuses will be needed?

Answer: _________

4. Oscar the rabbit was taken to the vets to be weighed. He weighed 1.8 kg.
A year later he was taken to the vets again. This time he weighed 300 g less.
How much did Oscar weigh on his second visit to the vets?
Circle the correct answer.

| | | | | | |
|---|---|---|---|---|---|
| **A** | 1500 kg | **C** | 150 g | **E** | 1.3 kg |
| **B** | 1.5 kg | **D** | 1800 g | | |

5. A sorting diagram is shown below.

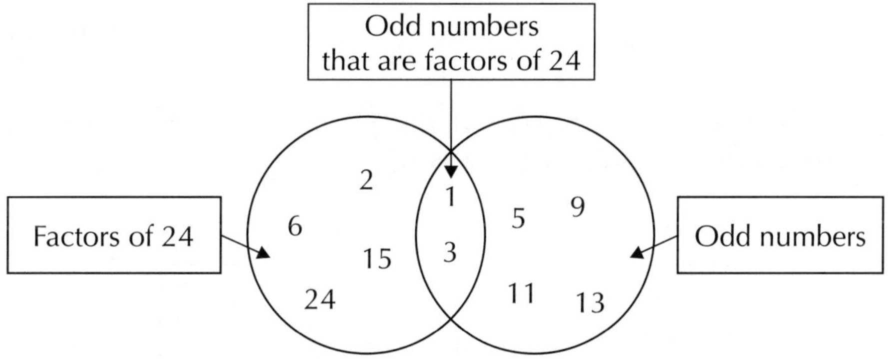


Which of these numbers is in the wrong place? Circle the correct answer.

**A** 15     **B** 24     **C** 9     **D** 13     **E** 1

6. A theatre ticket usually costs £40. For a popular show, the ticket prices are
increased by 20%. How much would a ticket cost for this show?

Answer: £ __________

7. What is the size of angle $x$ below?

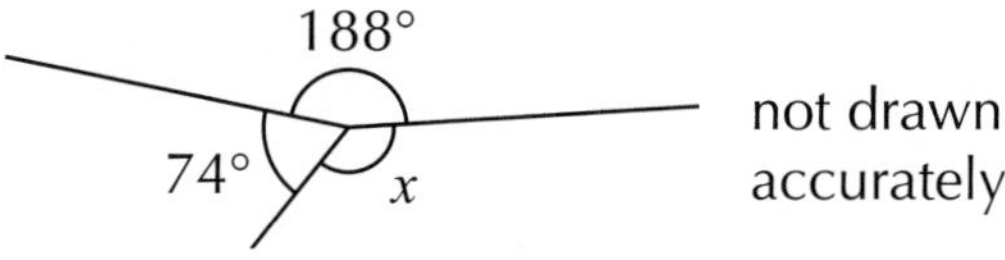


Answer: __________ °

8.  How many lines of symmetry does the following shape have?

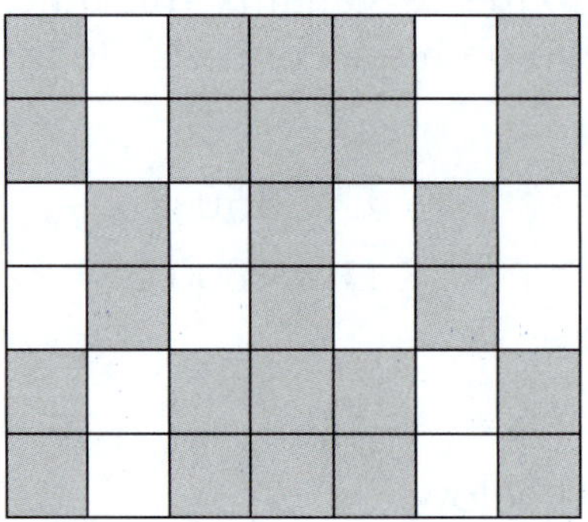

Answer: __________

9.  Bella makes a blanket by joining two identical squares of fabric together.
    Each fabric square has a perimeter of 40 cm.

Fabric square      Blanket 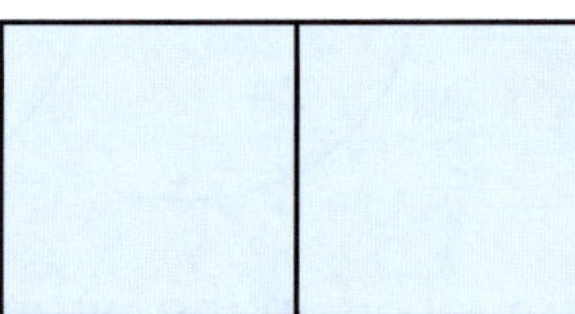

What is the perimeter of Bella's blanket?

Answer: __________ cm

10. Paula writes down the following equation.

$$X + Y = 11.5 - Y$$

If $X = 2.5$, what is $Y$ equal to?  Circle the correct answer.

**A**  2

**B**  4.5

**C**  9

**D**  1

**E**  11.5

/ 10



44

These puzzles are perfect for improving your **number** and **problem-solving** skills.

## Pancake Pilfering

When the pancakes are first served, Rachael has 10 pancakes, Steve has 2 pancakes and Tracy has none.

Every minute, Steve takes 3 pancakes from Rachael's plate, and Tracy takes 2 pancakes from Steve's plate.

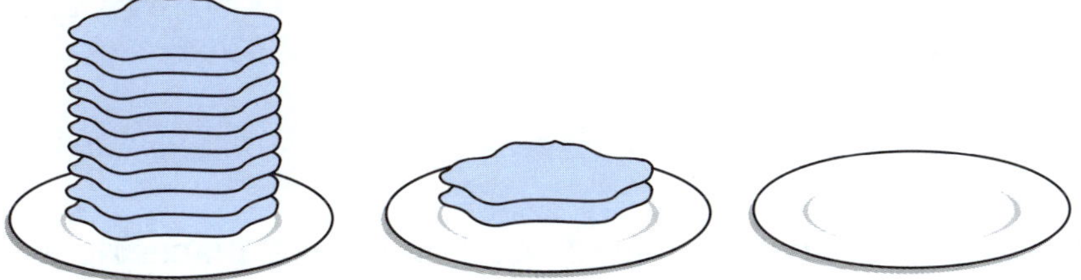

How many pancakes do they each have after 3 minutes?

Rachael: __________          Steve: __________          Tracy: __________

## The Old Couples' Bus Ride

Four old wives and their husbands went on a bus journey together.

Each wife sat next to a husband, but not their own husband.
- Mr Jones says, *"I didn't sit next to Mrs Smith or Mrs Brown."*
- Mrs Smith says, *"I didn't sit next to Mr MacDonald."*
- Mr MacDonald says, *"I didn't sit next to Mrs Jones."*

Use the information above to draw a line between each wife and the husband they sat next to.

| | |
|---|---|
| Mrs Jones | Mr Jones |
| Mrs Smith | Mr Smith |
| Mrs MacDonald | Mr MacDonald |
| Mrs Brown | Mr Brown |

# Test 14

You have **10 minutes** to do this test.  Work as quickly and accurately as you can.

1.  This is a train timetable from Benenden to Eton.

| Benenden | 08:00 | 08:45 | 09:30 | 10:15 |
|---|---|---|---|---|
| Chesterly | 08:20 | 09:05 | 09:50 | 10:35 |
| Eton | 08:35 | 09:20 | 10:05 | 10:50 |

Mei gets on the 08:45 train at Benenden.  How long is her train journey to Eton?

Answer: ___________ minutes

2.  Point P lies on a coordinate grid at (2, 7).  Point Q is 2 places right
and 4 places down from point P.  What are the coordinates of point Q?

Answer: ( ___________ , ___________ )

3.  Deshaun uses 250 g of cheese to make cheesy nachos for 8 people.
How much cheese would he need to make cheesy nachos for 40 people?
Circle the correct answer.

    **A**   1.5 kg        **C**   1250 g        **E**   2 kg

    **B**   12 500 g     **D**   12.5 kg

4.  How many edges does a triangular prism have?

Answer: ___________

5.    Max has a fair six-sided spinner, shown below.

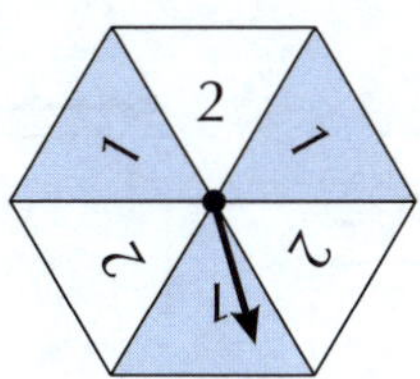

      What fraction of the spinner is shaded?  Circle the correct answer.

      **A**   $\frac{1}{2}$
      **B**   $\frac{1}{6}$
      **C**   $\frac{2}{3}$
      **D**   1
      **E**   $\frac{5}{6}$

6.    Use the calculation below to work out 24 × 1418.  Circle the correct answer.

      $$48 \times 1418 = 68\ 064$$

      **A**   34 064          **C**   136 128          **E**   241 418
      **B**   34 032          **D**   17 016

7.    Roz records the temperature in her garden at 8 pm every day for a week.
      The temperatures are listed below.

      | 0 °C | 7 °C | −3 °C | 0 °C | −4 °C | 7 °C | 0 °C |
      |---|---|---|---|---|---|---|

      Which of the following statements is true?  Circle the correct option.

      **A**   The temperature was below 0 °C on three different nights.
      **B**   The warmest night was 11 °C warmer than the coldest night.
      **C**   The most common temperature was 7 °C.
      **D**   The temperature was above 3 °C on three different nights.
      **E**   None of the above.

8.  A sequence of squares is shown below.  What is the area of Square 4?

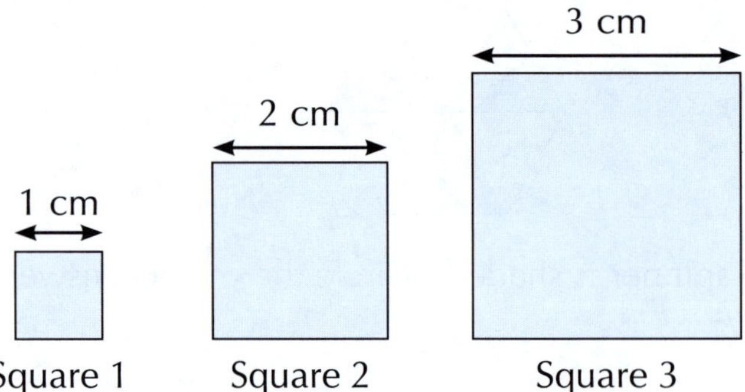


Answer: __________ cm$^2$

9.  Emily mixes 352 ml of orange juice, 230 ml of pineapple juice
    and 103 ml of grapefruit juice to make a fruit punch.
    How much fruit punch does she make in total?  Circle the correct answer.

    **A**   582 ml
    **B**   682 ml
    **C**   575 ml
    **D**   585 ml
    **E**   685 ml

10.  Kate spends £16.95 on food and £8.65 on drinks for a party.
     How much does she spend in total, to the nearest pound?
     Circle the correct answer.

    **A**   £26
    **B**   £25
    **C**   £30
    **D**   £20
    **E**   £27

/ 10

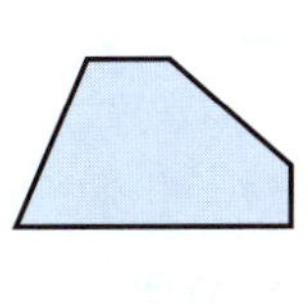

You have **10 minutes** to do this test.  Work as quickly and accurately as you can.

1.  Which two pentagons below are exactly the same shape?

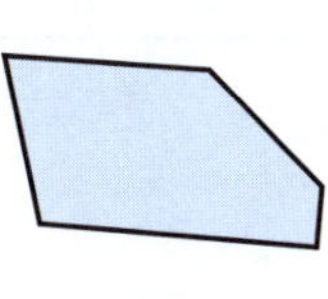 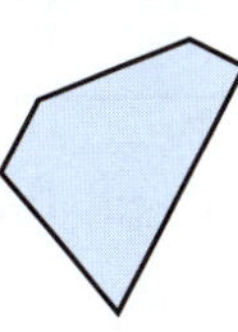 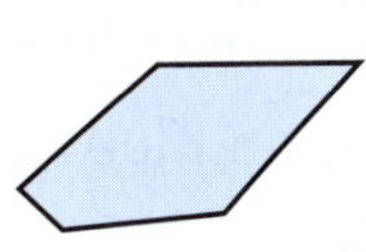 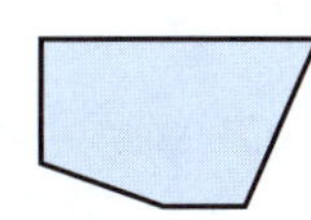

**A**          **B**          **C**          **D**          **E**

Answer: __________ and __________

2.  Kali doubles the largest prime number below 10.  What number does she get?

Answer: __________

3.  The time on Jane's digital clock reads 20:30.

Jane's alarm will go off at midnight.
How long will it be before her alarm goes off?

Answer: __________ hours, __________ minutes

4.  Yin is making a cup of tea.  Which of the following is the best estimate
for how much tea her cup can hold?  Circle the correct answer.

| | | |
|---|---|---|
| **A**  2.5 ml | **C**  25 000 ml | **E**  2500 l |
| **B**  25 l | **D**  250 ml | |

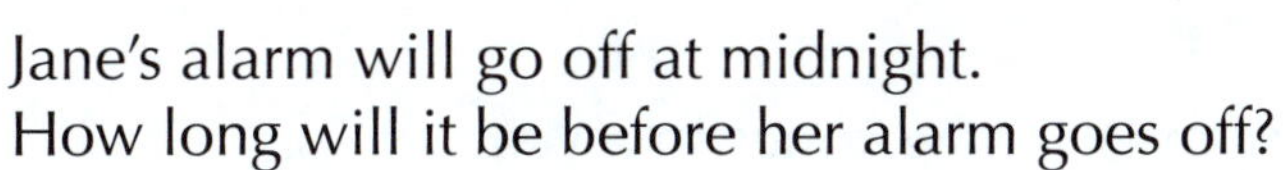

5.    Kleo is recording how many children in her class are right-handed or left-handed.
      Her results are shown in the table below.

|         | Right-handed | Left-handed | Total |
| ------- | ------------ | ----------- | ----- |
| **Boys**  | 12  |    | 14 |
| **Girls** | 11  | 5  | 16 |
| **Total** | 23  | 7  | 30 |

How many boys in Kleo's class are left-handed?

Answer: ___________

6.    Peter's phone bill (in £) is worked out using the formula $h + 5$,
      where $h$ = the number of hours Peter spends on the phone.
      If Peter spends 6 hours on the phone, how much will his phone bill be?

Answer: £___________

7.    Dominic wants to read 24 books and 10 magazines in a year.
      By the summer, he has read 1/4 of the books and 20% of the magazines.
      How many books and magazines does he have left to read?
      Circle the correct answer.

    **A**   18 books and 8 magazines
    **B**   6 books and 2 magazines
    **C**   18 books and 5 magazines
    **D**   6 books and 8 magazines
    **E**   19 books and 7 magazines

8. Only one of the statements below is true.  Circle the correct statement.

    **A**   $\frac{1}{4} = 0.4$

    **B**   $\frac{1}{3} > 0.5$

    **C**   $\frac{7}{10} = 0.75$

    **D**   $0.6 = \frac{3}{5}$

    **E**   $0.3 < \frac{3}{10}$

9. The pie charts below show how the students in two different classes get to school. Each class has 36 students.

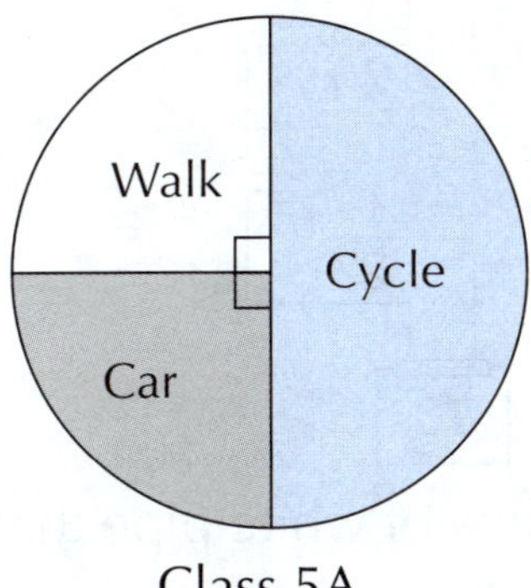


Class 5A

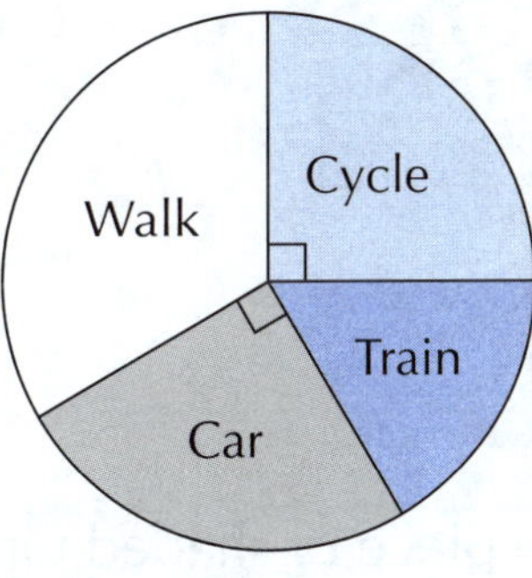


Class 5B

Which of these statements is false?  Circle the correct option.

    **A**   A quarter of all students in Class 5A walk to school.

    **B**   No students in Class 5A take the train to school.

    **C**   Twice as many students in Class 5A cycle to school as in Class 5B.

    **D**   More students in Class 5A walk to school than in Class 5B.

    **E**   Half of the students in Class 5A cycle to school.

10. Teo the dog eats 400 g of dog food each day.  Dog food is sold in 6 kg bags. How many days will one bag of dog food last?

Answer: ____________

/ 10

**Addition** and knowing your **units** will help with these puzzles.  Mathematical!

# Pipe Swap

Plumber Jane is having problems with some pipes.
The shaded pipes and the white pipes need to add up to the same value.

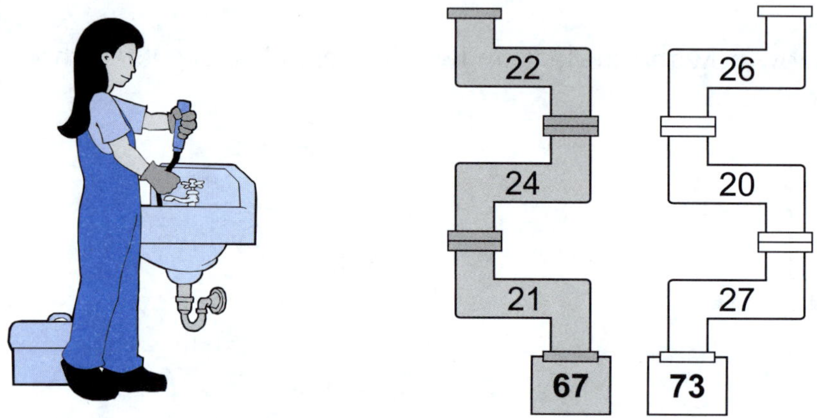


Circle one piece of shaded pipe and one piece of white pipe that should be swapped, so that the totals are equal.

# The Wag Swag Bag Snag

Wag Swag sells a selection of dog-related items.

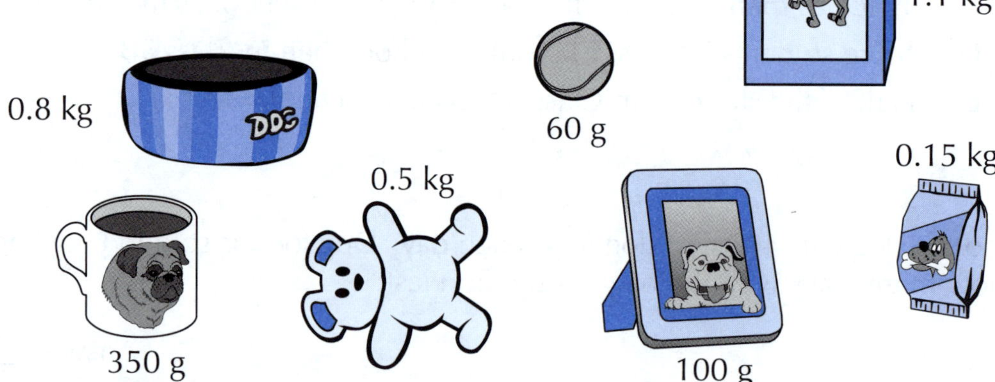


Doug's bag can hold 1.2 kg before it tears.  He puts 3 different items in his bag and it doesn't tear.  What's the heaviest his bag could be?

_____________ kg

 

10

You have **10 minutes** to do this test.  Work as quickly and accurately as you can.

1.  Kirsty draws a shape on the coordinate grid below.

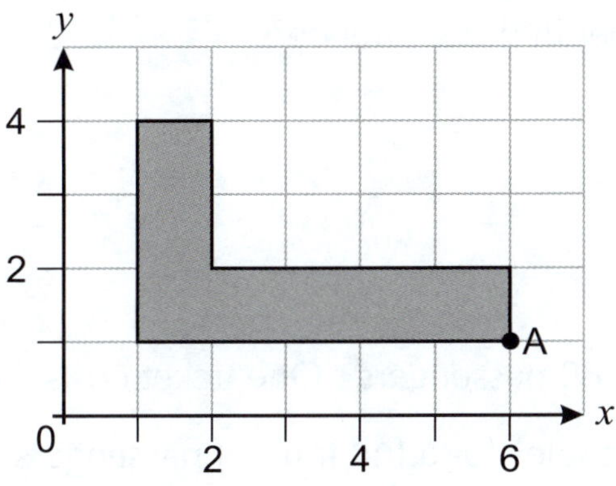

What are the coordinates of point A?

Answer: ( _________ , _________ )

2.  How many obtuse angles are shown in total on the two shapes below?

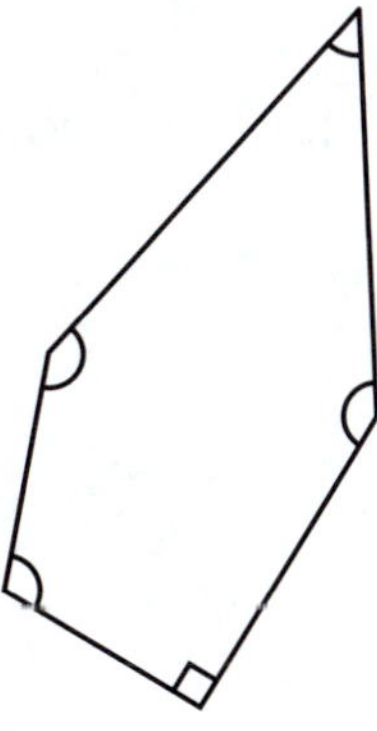 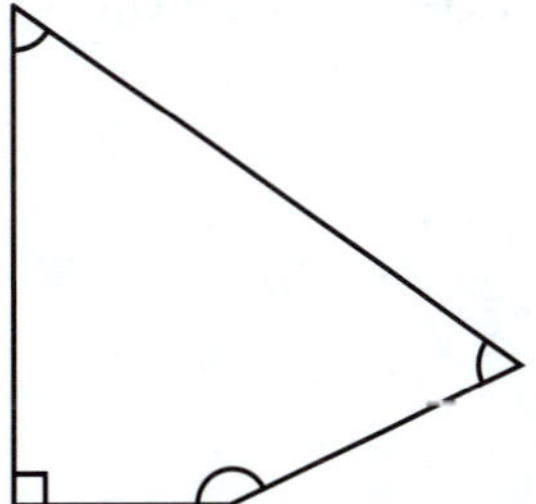

Answer: _________

3.  Roopesh divides a bag of sugar into 20 equal piles.  Each pile weighs 75 g.
    What was the total weight of his bag of sugar?  Circle the correct answer.

| | | |
|---|---|---|
| **A**  5 kg | **C**  1.5 kg | **E**  1.5 g |
| **B**  0.75 kg | **D**  0.75 g | |

4.  Paul is given the sequence of numbers shown below.  To get the next number
    in the sequence, he must add the last two numbers in the sequence.

| 1 | 1 | 2 | 3 | 5 | ? |

What is the next number in the sequence?

Answer: _____________

5.  A train can carry up to 80 passengers.  One ticket costs £4.95.

Estimate the total ticket sales for a full train of passengers.
Circle the correct answer.

**A**   £800          **C**   £1600          **E**   £40

**B**   £320          **D**   £400

6.  Joel invited 20 people to a party.  $^1/_{10}$ of the people Joel invited didn't go.
    How many of those invited did go to Joel's party?

Answer: _____________

7.  Zac writes down all the factors of 36.  Which number is he missing?

1   2   3   4   6   12   18   36

Answer: _____________

8. Libby draws a pie chart to record the number of different coloured pebbles she finds on a beach one day.

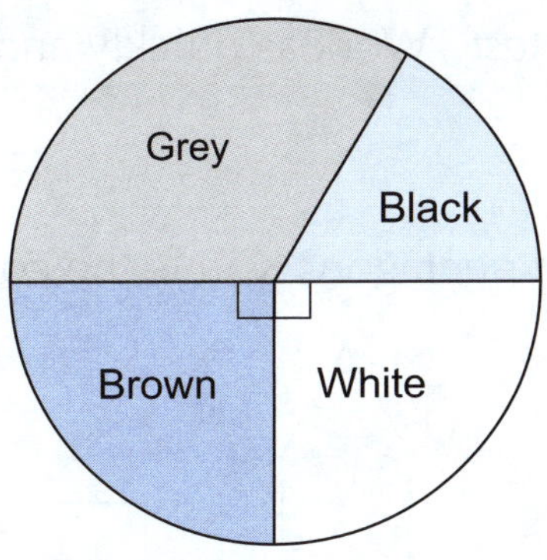


Libby found 36 black and grey pebbles in total.
How many brown pebbles did she find?

Answer: _____________

9. Conor thinks of a number.  He adds two and then doubles it.
He ends up with 44.  What number did Conor think of?

Answer: _____________

10. Leigh has a bag of 10 sweets.  7 sweets are red.  3 sweets are blue.
Leigh eats a red sweet.  What fraction of sweets in the bag are now red?
Circle the correct answer.

    **A** $^7/_{10}$          **C** $^6/_7$          **E** $^1/_3$

    **B** $^3/_{10}$          **D** $^2/_3$

/ 10





Test 16

You have **10 minutes** to do this test.  Work as quickly and accurately as you can.

1.  Which of the following is a pentagon?  Circle the correct option.

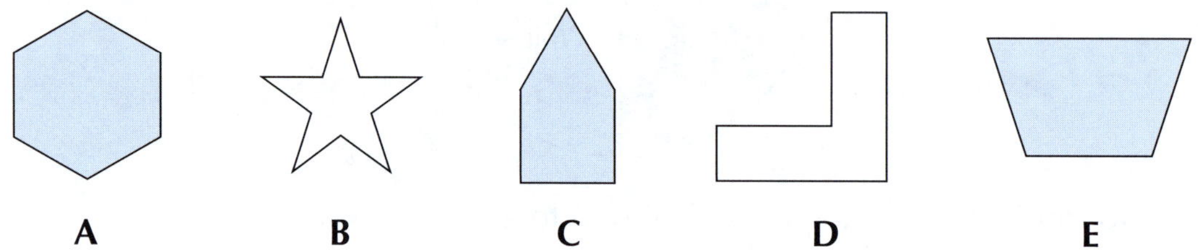

**A**  **B**  **C**  **D**  **E**

2.  The Number Cruncher uses a formula to turn one number into another.

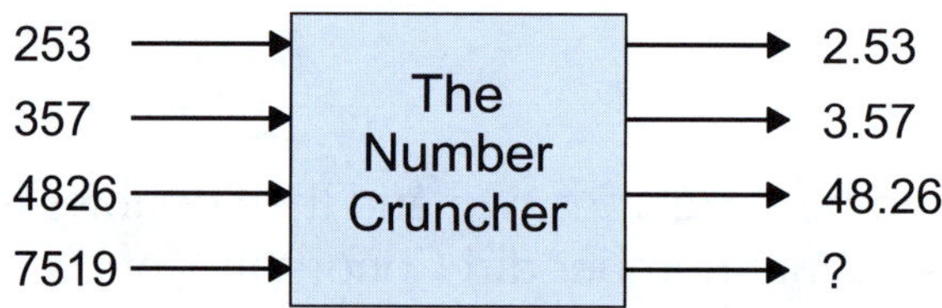

When you put 7519 in The Number Cruncher, what comes out?
Circle the correct option.

| | | |
|---|---|---|
| **A**  7.519 | **C**  75.19 | **E**  7519 |
| **B**  751.9 | **D**  0.7519 | |

3.  Which of these statements is false?  Circle the correct option.

**A**  All angles in a rectangle are right-angles.

**B**  Opposite sides of a rectangle are parallel.

**C**  A rectangle always has four lines of symmetry.

**D**  Opposite sides of a rectangle are equal in length.

**E**  A rectangle is a quadrilateral.

4.    Talat is in a band.  He records how many people download
      his album each month in the bar chart below.

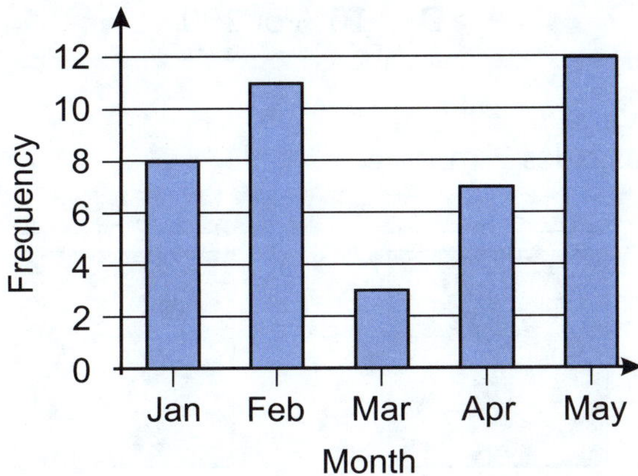


How many more albums were downloaded in May than in March?

Answer: ___________

5.    Ana grows strawberries and sells them for £1.50 per bag.  Each bag contains 500 g
      of strawberries.  How much money does Ana make if she sells 3 kg of strawberries?

Answer: £___________

6.    Caitlin's watch is shown below.  It is running 25 minutes behind the actual time.

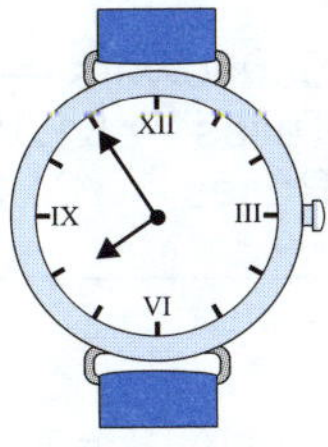


Given that it is morning, what is the actual time?

Answer: ___________ : ___________ am

7. Which of the following gives the largest answer?  Circle the correct option.

    **A**   $100 \div 4$         **C**   $10 \times 2$         **E**   $0.5 \times 100$

    **B**   $\frac{1}{10}$ of 100       **D**   10% of 200

8. A square tabletop has sides 2 m long.

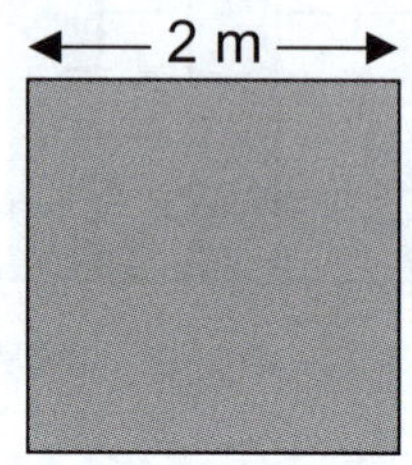


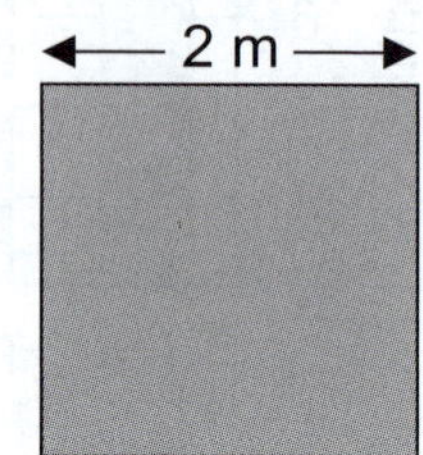


If two identical square tables are pushed together,
what is the perimeter of the new tabletop?

Answer: ___________ m

9. The first four terms in a sequence are 20.2, 19.8, 19.4, 19.0.
What is the next term in the sequence?

Answer: ___________

10. Holly's Florist sells many different flowers.

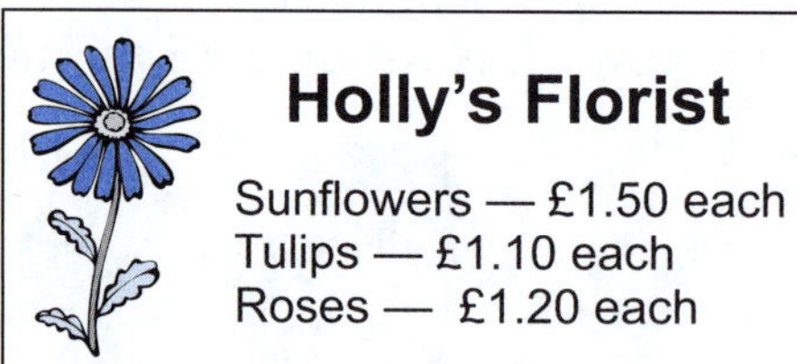


Astrid buys 2 roses and 1 tulip.
How much change does she get from a £5 note?

Answer: £___________

/ 10

You have **10 minutes** to do this test.  Work as quickly and accurately as you can.

1.　Leo runs 9392 metres.  How far does he run to the nearest hundred metres?

Answer: ___________ m

2.　Tim buys a 1500 ml tin of paint.  He needs 1.8 litres to paint a wall.
　　How much more paint does he need?

Answer: __________ ml

3.　This diagram shows Rosa's pond.

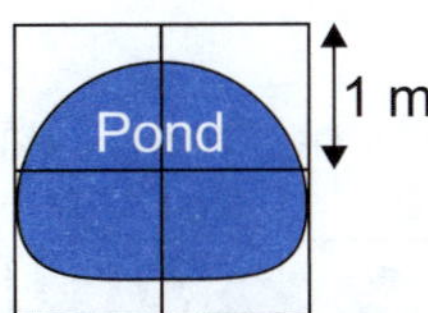


　　Which of these is true about the area of her pond?  Circle the correct answer.

    **A**　The area of her pond is less than 1 m².

    **B**　The area of her pond is more than 4 m².

    **C**　The area of her pond is exactly 1 m².

    **D**　The area of her pond is less than 4 m².

    **E**　The area of her pond is exactly 8 m².

4.   A cinema is showing the film 'The Odd Ghost'.
The film is 2 hours and 45 minutes long.
If it starts at 5:20 pm, what time will the film finish?

Answer: __________ : __________ pm

5.   Larry has a herd of llamas.  The oldest llama is 12 years and 2 months old.
The youngest is 6 months old.  What is the difference in their ages?

Answer: __________ years, __________ months

6.   A skeleton is on display in a museum.  The skull of the skeleton is $\frac{1}{5}$ of the height
of the whole skeleton.  If the whole skeleton is 150 cm tall, how tall is the skull?

Answer: __________ cm

7.   Eli records the number of cookies his family eats each day in the pictogram below.

| Friday | ◓ ◓ ◓ ◓ |
|---|---|
| Saturday | ◓ ◓ ◓ |
| Sunday | ◓ ◓ |

Eight fewer cookies were eaten on Sunday than on Friday.
Which number replaces the '?' in the key?

Answer: __________

8.  Which of these numbers is closest to 10?  Circle the correct answer.

    **A**   9.92            **C**   9.5            **E**   10.1

    **B**   10.25          **D**   10.05

9.  A sequence starts 2, 4, 8, 16, ...
    Each term is found by doubling the previous term.

    Which of these numbers does not appear in the sequence?
    Circle the correct option.

    **A**   64       **B**   32       **C**   28       **D**   256       **E**   128

10.  Isla draws a 4 cm square and a 3 cm square, as shown below.

What is the difference in the areas of the squares?

Answer: _________ cm$^2$

/ 10

Puzzle time!  These puzzles are a great way to practise **directions** and **sequences**.

# Greybeard's Treasure

Greybeard has buried some treasure on an island.  Using the directions below, work out where his treasure can be found.  Mark it with an **X** on the map.

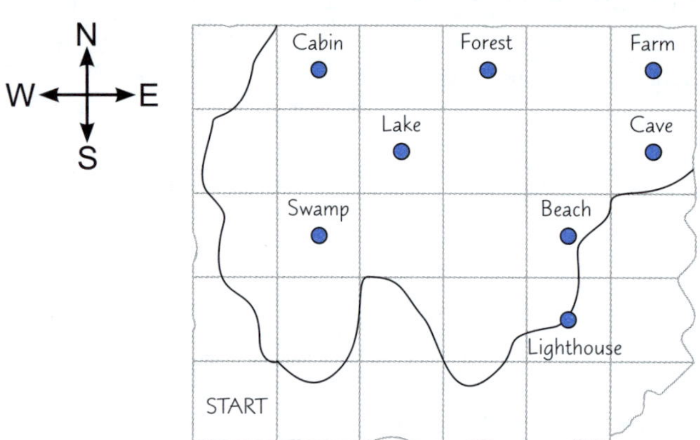


1)   Start on the bottom-left square, facing **North.**

2)   Turn **90° clockwise,** then move forward **2 squares.**

3)   Turn **90° anticlockwise,** then move forward **3 squares.**

4)   Turn **180° clockwise,** then move forward **1 square.**

5)   Turn **90° anticlockwise,** then move forward **2 squares.**

# Zoo-sual Suspects

These animals are part of a sequence.

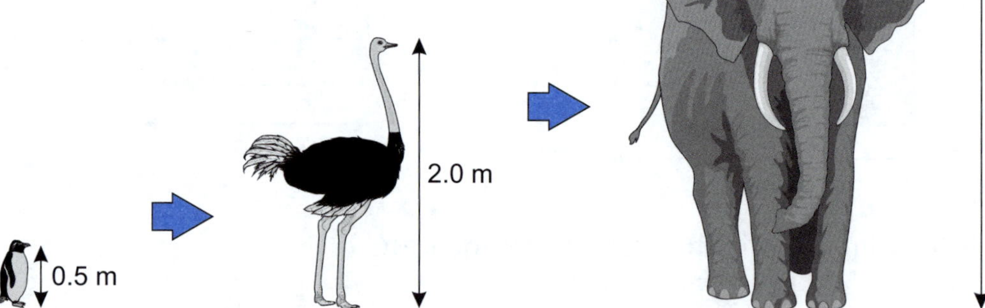


How tall is the next animal in the sequence?

______________ m

Which animal could be next in the sequence?  Circle the correct option.

*Lion*          *Giraffe*          *Peacock*          *Zebra*          *Monkey*

(10)

You have **10 minutes** to do this test.  Work as quickly and accurately as you can.

1.    What fraction of the shape below is shaded?

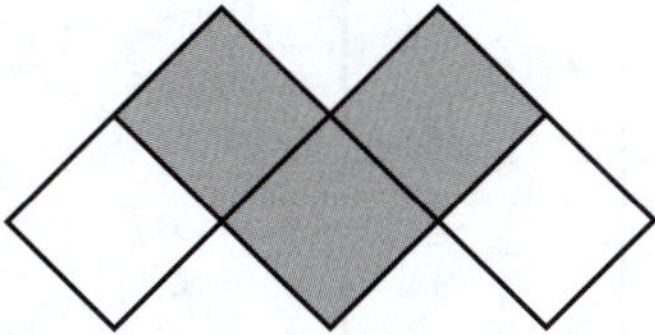

Answer: ___________

2.    Mr Egbert wants to measure the height of a kettle.
      What would be the most sensible units to use?  Circle the correct answer.

   **A**   mm          **B**   cm          **C**   m          **D**   g          **E**   km

3.    Toby types a story that is 400 words long.  10% of all the words he types
      are spelt wrong.  How many words are spelt wrong in Toby's story?

Answer: ___________

4.    A group of children were asked which pet they would most like to own
      from a choice of five.  The results are shown on the bar chart below.

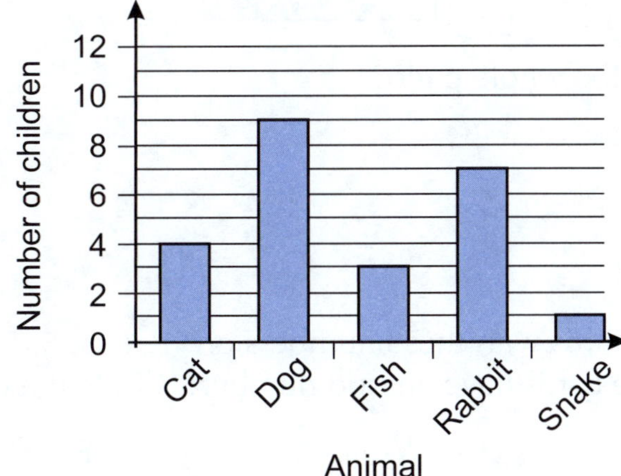


How many more children said they would prefer a rabbit than a fish?

Answer: ___________

5.    On the coordinate grid is a point labelled A, and a mirror line.

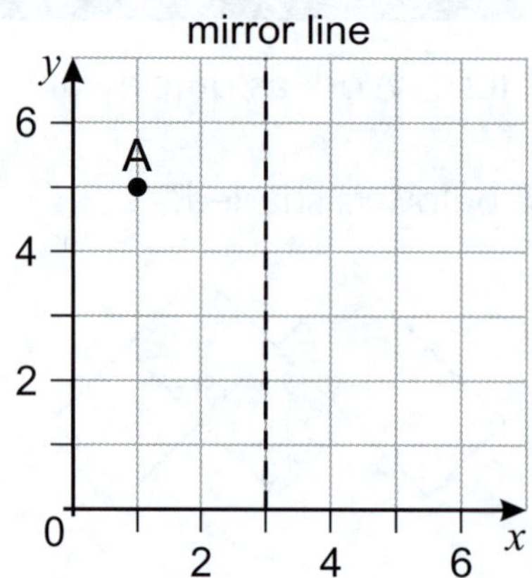



Point A is reflected in the mirror line.  What are the new coordinates of point A?

Answer: ( ___________ , ___________ )

6.    A patio is made by arranging four identical rectangles and a square, shown below.

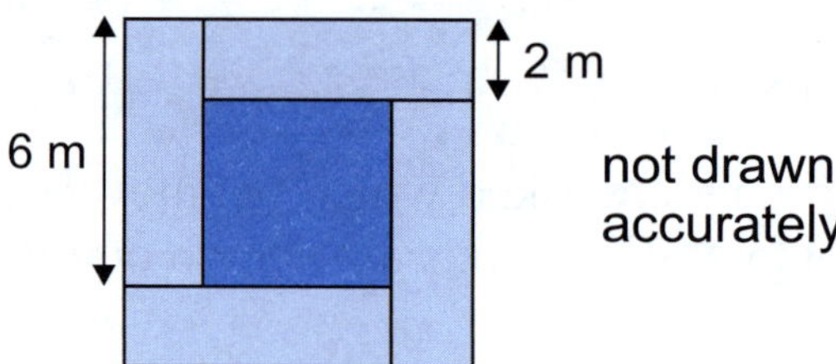



What is the area of the whole patio?

Answer: ___________ m²

7.    A bag contains six cards with these numbers on: 1, 1, 3, 5, 5 and 6.
      What fraction of the cards have an odd number?  Circle the correct option.

   **A**   $^1/_6$                **C**   $^1/_3$                **E**   $^5/_6$
   **B**   $^1/_2$                **D**   1

8.  An artist starts a painting on the 8th February.  He finishes the painting on the 27th of the same month.  How many weeks and days did it take to finish the painting?

Answer: ___________ weeks, ___________ days

9.  Two gymnasts took part in a competition.  Here are their results.

| Name | Skills | Difficulty | Mistakes | Score |
| --- | --- | --- | --- | --- |
| Maria | 5 | 3.0 | 2.5 | |
| Yaling | 5 | 4.0 | 4.5 | 9.5 |

The score is calculated by doubling the number in the skills column, adding the number in the difficulty column and then subtracting the number in the mistakes column.

What is Maria's score?

Answer: ___________

10.  Meera has found that if you add all the factors of 28, apart from itself, it equals itself.

$$28 = 1 + 2 + 4 + 7 + 14$$

For which of the following numbers does this also work?  Circle the correct option.

| | | |
| --- | --- | --- |
| **A**   2 | **C**   6 | **E**   10 |
| **B**   4 | **D**   8 | |

/ 10





Test 19

You have **10 minutes** to do this test.  Work as quickly and accurately as you can.

1.  A blue whale is 30 m long.  How long is the blue whale in centimetres?
    Circle the correct answer.

|  |  |  |
|---|---|---|
| **A**  0.3 cm | **C**  300 cm | **E**  300 000 cm |
| **B**  0.03 cm | **D**  3000 cm | |

2.  Karl counts backwards from 13, subtracting 6 each time.
    What is the first negative number he gets to?

    Answer: – ___________

3.  A teddy bear costs £5.95.  How many teddy bears can Eimear buy with a £20 note?

    Answer: ___________

4.  Two angles lie at a point on a straight line.  What is angle $x$ in the diagram below?

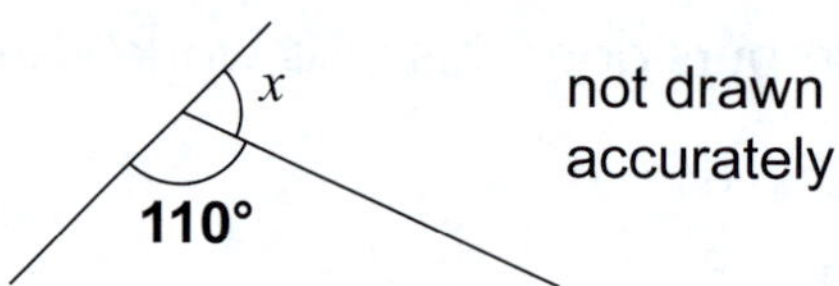


    Answer: ___________ °

5.    How many lines of symmetry does this shape have?

Answer: __________


6.    This table shows the times of five swimmers who took part in a 50 m race.

| Swimmer | Cynthia | Melissa | Eva | Joan | Lin |
|---------|---------|---------|------|------|------|
| Time (s) | 35.4 | 33.2 | 45.9 | 31.4 | 40.0 |

What was the time difference between the fastest and slowest swimmer?

Answer: __________ s


7.    A line graph shows the number of hours that
two cats, Ziggy and Mylo, sleep in a day.

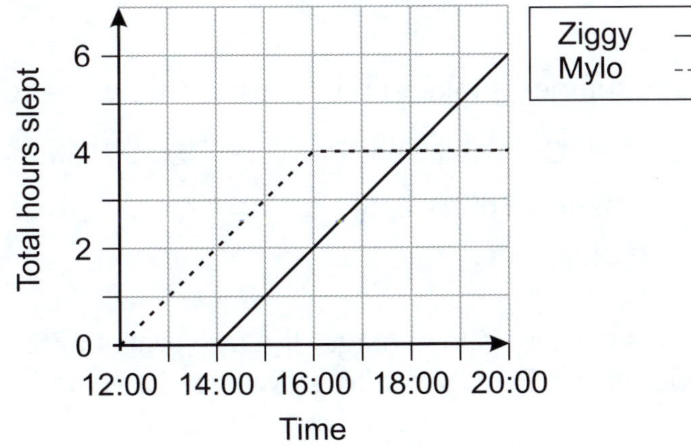

At what time had the cats slept for the same total number of hours?

Answer: __________ : __________

8.    The volume of the box below is 20 cm$^3$.

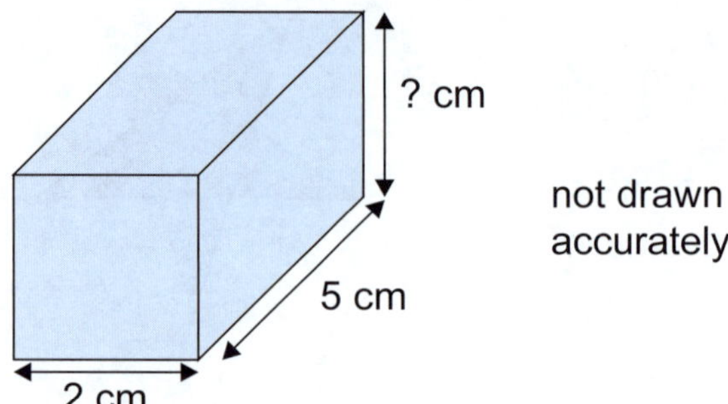


What is the length of the missing side?

Answer: ___________ cm

9.    This fair five-sector spinner is used to predict
the weather in Grimwich on any one day.

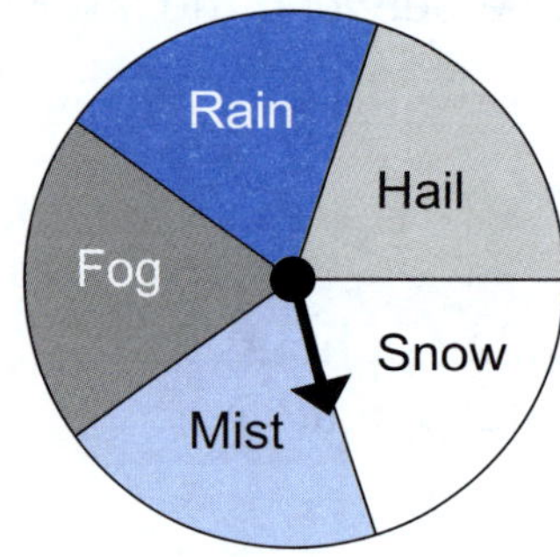


What percentage of the spinner is taken up by 'mist'?  Circle the correct answer.

| | | |
|---|---|---|
| **A**   20% | **C**   10% | **E**   25% |
| **B**   50% | **D**   80% | |

10.   Percy plants a tree in his garden.  On average, the tree grows 27 cm each year.
How much would you expect Percy's tree to grow over 12 years?

Answer: ___________ cm

/ 10

Time for a break!  These puzzles focus on **multiplication** and **addition**.

## Wires Gone Haywire

Four bulbs are connected to plugs A to D.  The value on each plug multiplied by the bulb they are connected to should give 36.
Two of the bulbs are connected to the wrong plugs.

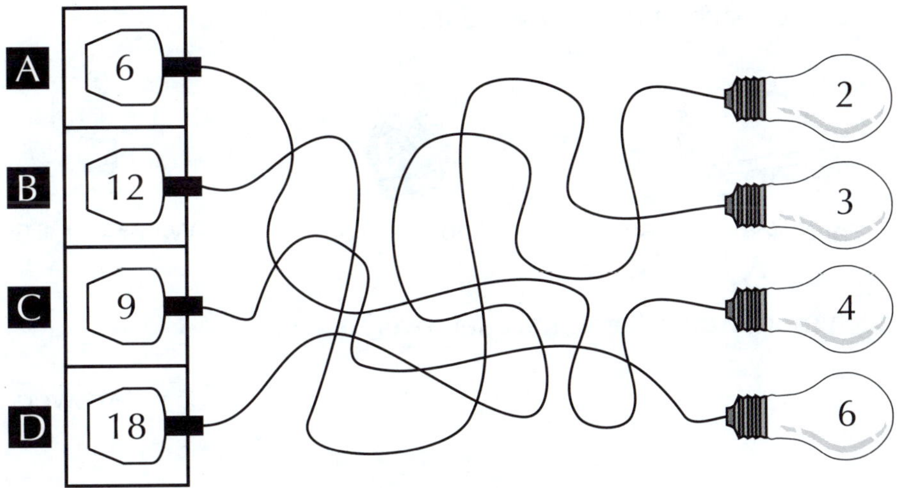


Which two plugs have a wrong bulb attached?

______________ and ______________

## Connie's Coin Conundrum

Connie has six coins: 1p, 2p, 5p, 10p, 20p and 50p.  Connie wants to buy one keyring using exactly the right amount of money.  Circle the keyring she can buy.

  69  

10

You have **10 minutes** to do this test.  Work as quickly and accurately as you can.

1.    A square has a side length of 7 cm.  What is its perimeter?

Answer: _____________ cm

2.    Sarah is buying her lunch.  She has £12 to spend.
      She buys one of each of the following items.

Sandwich — £5.50

Apple — 75p

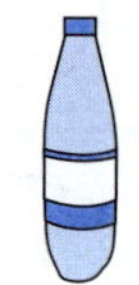

Water — £1.50

How much money does Sarah have left over?

Answer: £ ___________

3.    Jack draws a shape on some dotted paper, shown here.

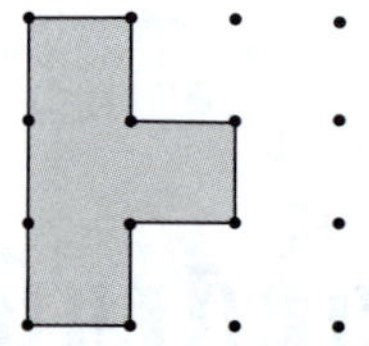

Which of these shapes has the same area as Jack's shape?
Circle the correct answer.

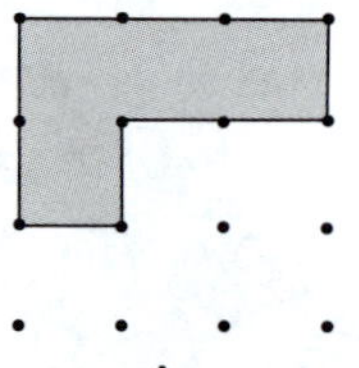

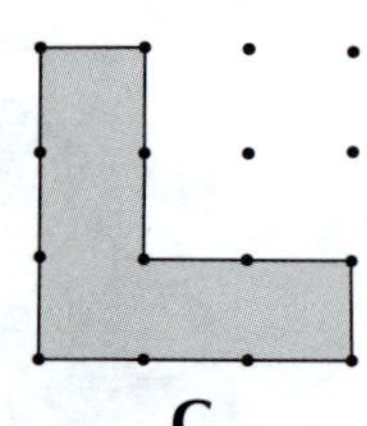

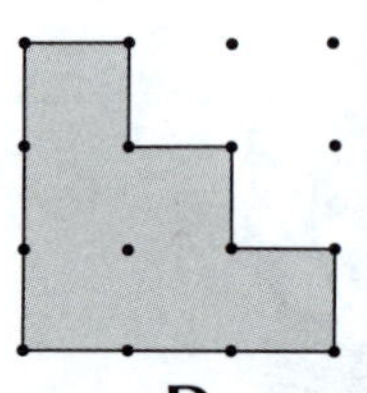

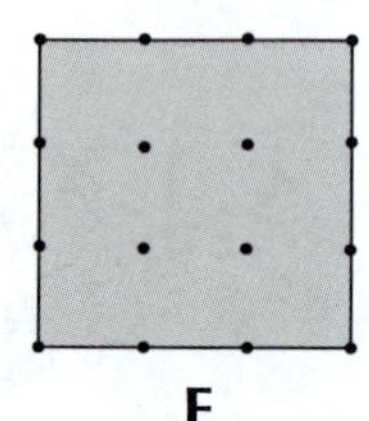

A          B          C          D          E

4.  Barry is mixing concrete.  He starts by pouring 3 litres of water into a bucket.
Each litre of water weighs 1 kg and the empty bucket weighs 500 g.

What is the total weight of the bucket filled with the water?
Give your answer in grams.

Answer: ___________ g


5.  Fatima starts at 10 and counts back in steps of 4.
What number does she have after three steps?  Circle the correct answer.

**A**   −14        **C**   −2        **E**   −6
**B**   0          **D**   −10


6.  The bar chart below shows the number of people who
went for a haircut at Safia's Barbershop last week.

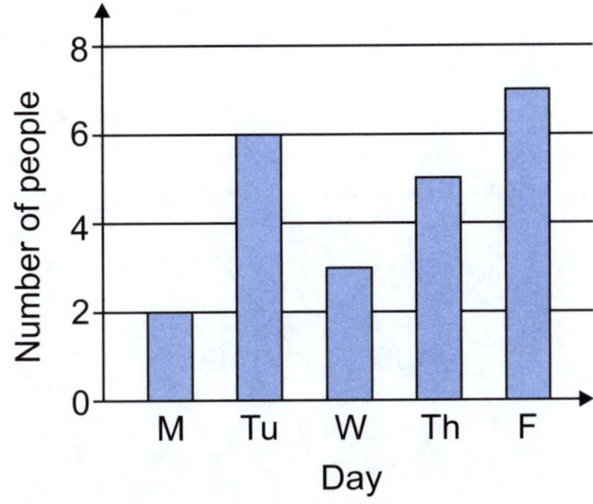


Between which two days was there the greatest difference in the number
of people who went for a haircut?  Circle the correct answer.

**A**   Monday and Tuesday
**B**   Monday and Thursday
**C**   Monday and Friday
**D**   Tuesday and Wednesday
**E**   Wednesday and Thursday

7.  Which of the options below will equal 500?  Circle the correct answer.

    **A**    487 rounded to the nearest 10

    **B**    599 rounded to the nearest 100

    **C**    525 rounded to the nearest 1000

    **D**    506 rounded to the nearest 10

    **E**    453 rounded to the nearest 100

8.  What is the volume of this cuboid?

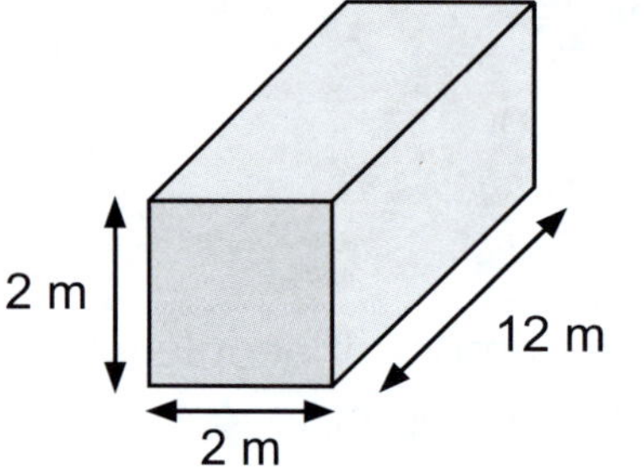


Answer: __________ m³

9.  Find the size of angle $x$, shown below.

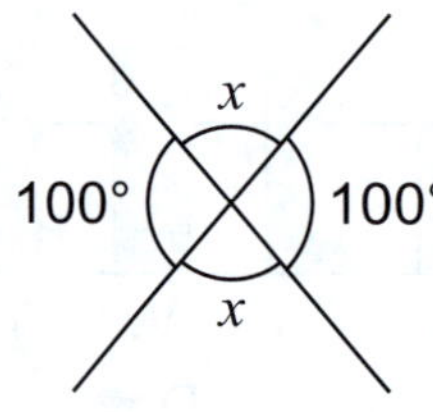


Answer: __________ °

10. April played 20 games in a chess tournament.  She lost $^1/_4$, drew 10%,
    and won the rest.  How many games did she win?

Answer: __________

/ 10

You have **10 minutes** to do this test.  Work as quickly and accurately as you can.

1.  Three thousand, five hundred and eight people attended the Grizebeck rock festival last year.  What is this number in figures?

Answer: ___________

2.  A pencil is measured against a centimetre ruler, as shown in the diagram.

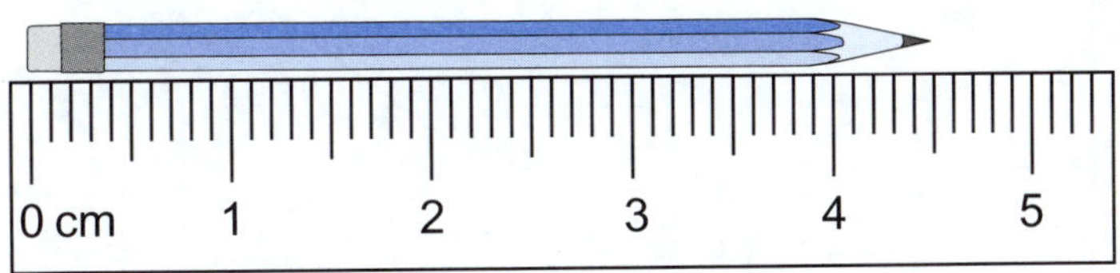


Using the diagram, how long is the pencil in millimetres?

Answer: ___________ mm

3.  Which number correctly completes the following calculation?

$$10 + 10 + 10 = 6 \times \underline{\hspace{2em}}$$

Answer: ___________

4.  This diagram shows point S and point T.

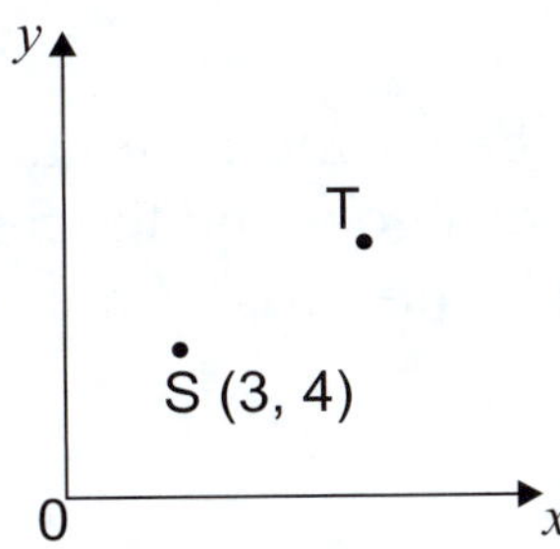


Which of these could be the coordinates of point T?  Circle the correct answer.

| | | |
|---|---|---|
| **A**  (2, 3) | **C**  (–1, 6) | **E**  (1, 8) |
| **B**  (8, 7) | **D**  (9, 4) | |

5.  A bottle of milk holds 500 ml and costs 60p.  Nathan buys 3 l of milk.
    How much does this cost him?

Answer: £__________

6.  An online computer game lets you convert real money into virtual money to use in
    the game.  The graph shown converts real pounds (£) into virtual dollars ($).

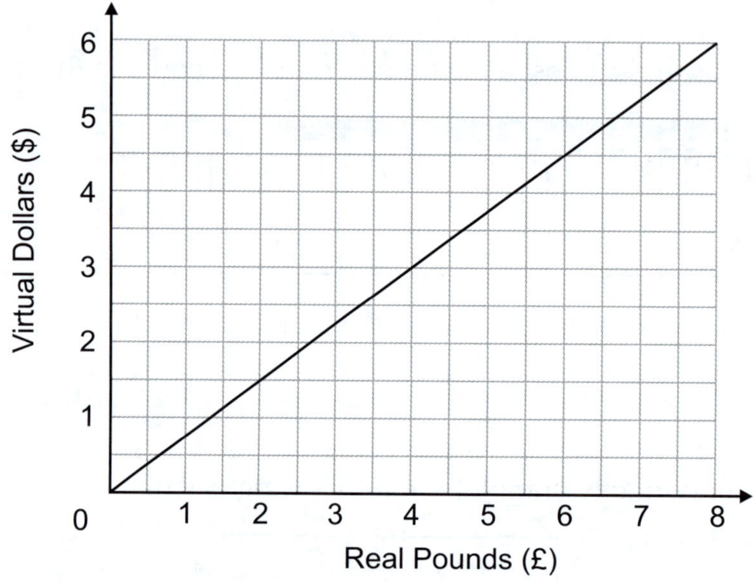


Jessica converts 4 real pounds (£) into virtual dollars ($).
How many virtual dollars ($) does she receive?

Answer: $__________

7.  A class of 20 children choose their favourite fruit.  $^1/_{10}$ of the children
    choose bananas, 20% choose mangoes and the rest choose oranges.
    What is the most popular fruit in the class?  Circle the correct answer.

    **A**   Oranges

    **B**   Mangoes

    **C**   Bananas

    **D**   Both mangoes and oranges

    **E**   Impossible to tell

8.  Matthew and Rebecca have a combined age of 33.
    Rebecca is 3 years older than Matthew.  How old is Matthew?

Answer: __________

9.  Look at the diagram below.

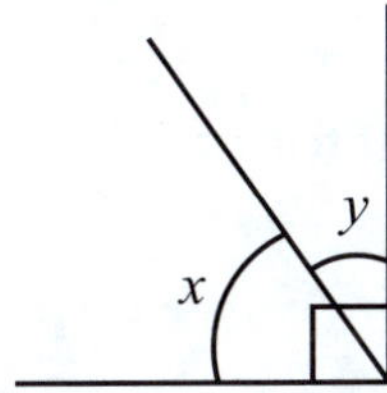


Which expression correctly describes the angles shown?  Circle the correct option.

**A**  $x - y = 90°$
**B**  $x + x = 45°$
**C**  $x + y = 45°$
**D**  $x + y = 90°$
**E**  $2x + y = 180°$

10. Theo works at Preston station.  He notices that the Manchester train enters the
    station every 2 hours and the Birmingham train enters the station every 3 hours.
    At 07:00, Theo watches the two trains both enter the station at the same time.

    What time will the two trains next enter the station at the same time?
    Give your answer in 24-hour clock format.

Answer: __________ : __________

/ 10

You have **10 minutes** to do this test.  Work as quickly and accurately as you can.

1.   What is $36 - (7 \times 2)$?

Answer:  ___________

2.   Which of the following numbers is not a factor of 24?
Circle the correct answer.

   **A**   5            **C**   2            **E**   6

   **B**   3            **D**   4

3.   This chart shows the population of different types of butterfly in a butterfly house.

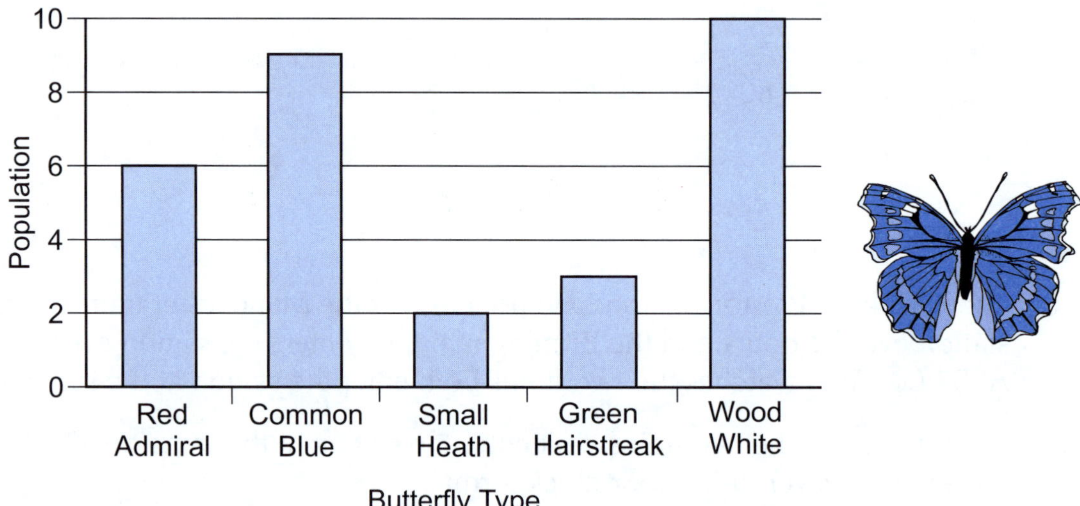


Which butterfly type has a population that is $^1/_3$ of the
Common Blue population?  Circle the correct answer.

   **A**   Red Admiral         **C**   Green Hairstreak         **E**   None of them

   **B**   Small Heath          **D**   Wood White

4.  Each book in a second-hand bookshop costs 80p.
    Damon has a £5 note.  How many books can he buy?

Answer: __________

5.  Jayden makes 8 carrot cakes to sell at a fair.  Each cake weighs 350 g.
    What is the total weight of all the carrot cakes Jayden made?

Answer: __________ g

6.  What is the perimeter of the shape below?

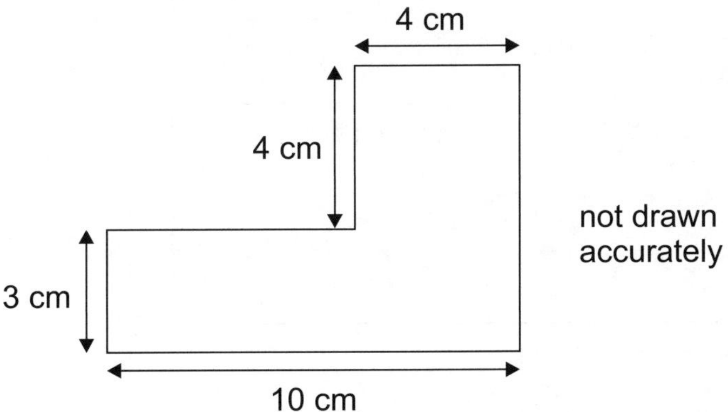


Answer: __________ cm

7.  Noam has six coffee mugs.
    The size of each of his mugs is shown below.

| 275 ml | 350 ml | 425 ml | 300 ml | 360 ml | 200 ml |

Noam fills the smallest coffee mug to the top with coffee.
He then pours 25% of this coffee into another mug.
How much coffee is left in the smallest mug?  Circle the correct option.

A   100 ml          C   225 ml          E   175 ml
B   250 ml          D   150 ml

8. Zara is a policewoman.  In week 1, she caught 3 criminals.
In week 2, she caught 6 criminals.  In week 3, she caught 9 criminals.

If the number of criminals she catches keeps increasing at the same rate,
how many criminals will Zara catch in week 5?

Answer: __________

9. The diagram below shows a car park and an office building.

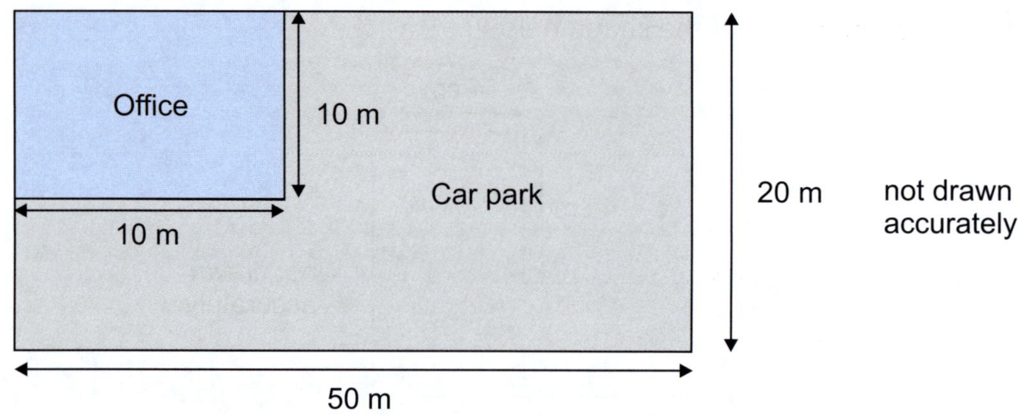


What is the total area of the car park?

Answer: __________ m²

10. Gurinda is making a patio.  She needs 30 patio slabs.
5 patio slabs cost £20.  How much will 30 patio slabs cost?

Answer: £__________

/ 10

Have a go at these puzzles — they're ideal for practising **problem-solving** skills.

## Sheep Separation

A farmer has painted all of her sheep with a number. By drawing no more than three straight lines, divide her sheep into five different groups, so that the numbers on the sheep in each group add up to the same value.

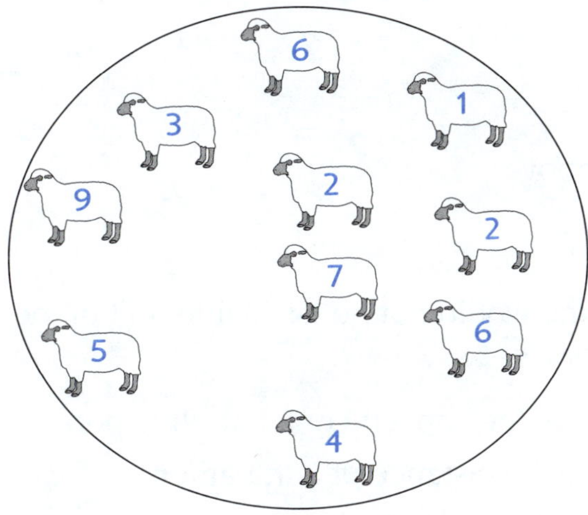


## Shape Selection

Lucy, Martin, Nathan and Olivia choose their favourite shape below. They each chose a different shape.

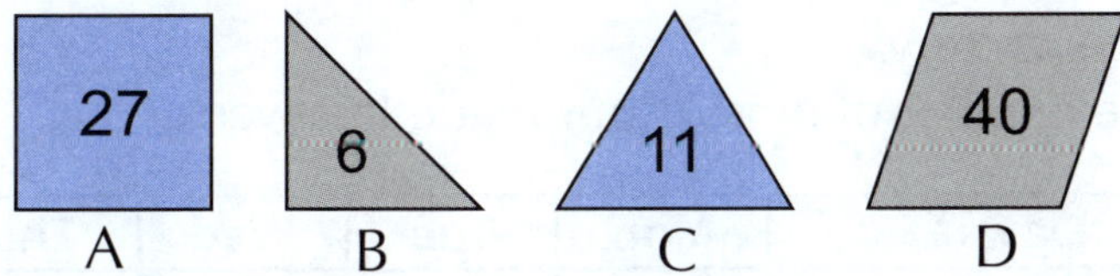


Lucy says, *"My shape has at least two right angles."*

Martin says, *"My shape has an even number on it."*

Nathan says, *"My shape is blue."*

Olivia says, *"My shape is a triangle."*

Use the information above to write the correct letter next to each name.

Lucy: __________     Martin: __________     Nathan: __________     Olivia: __________

# Test 24

You have **10 minutes** to do this test.  Work as quickly and accurately as you can.

1.  Caspar is standing on the top of a mountain, facing north.
    Which direction will he face if he turns 90° anticlockwise?
    Circle the correct answer.

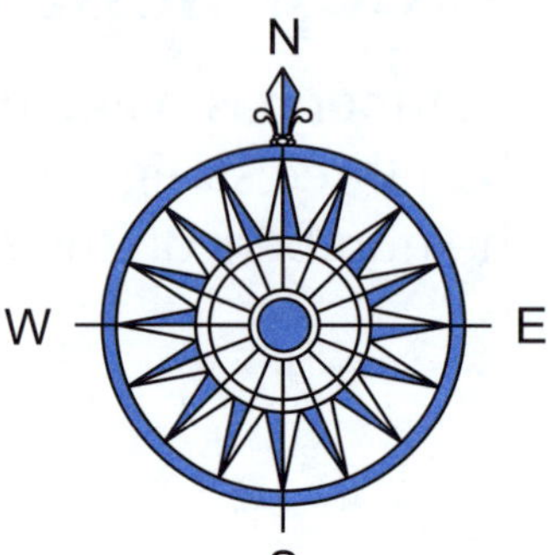

    **A**   North

    **B**   West

    **C**   East

    **D**   South

    **E**   None of the above

2.  Which of the following would not be a suitable unit of measurement?
    Circle the correct answer.

    **A**   litres to measure the capacity of a paddling pool.

    **B**   km to measure the distance of a marathon.

    **C**   g to measure the weight of a loaf of bread.

    **D**   $m^2$ to measure the area of a football pitch.

    **E**   mm to measure the distance between Earth and the Moon.

3.  Arthur works in a pin factory.
    The table shows the number of pins Arthur made last week.

| Day | Mon | Tue | Wed | Thu | Fri |
|---|---|---|---|---|---|
| Number of push pins | 500 | 300 | 200 | 400 | 700 |
| Number of safety pins | 200 | 400 | 600 | 500 | 100 |

On which day did Arthur make the most pins?  Circle the correct answer.

    **A**   Monday       **C**   Wednesday       **E**   Friday

    **B**   Tuesday       **D**   Thursday

4.  A supermarket sells bread in whole loaves and half loaves.
A whole loaf costs £1.20.  Ellie buys one whole loaf and three half loaves.
She pays £3.00.  How much does a half loaf cost?

Answer: £ __________

5.  Mrs Thomas asks all the children in her class what their favourite holiday is.
She shows her results using the chart below.

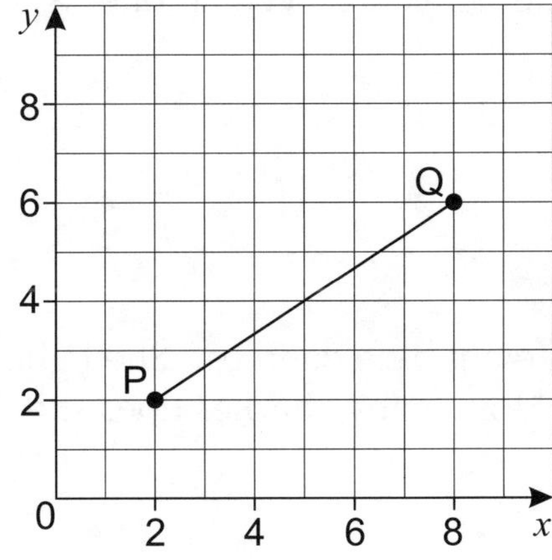

What percentage of her class say Easter is their favourite holiday?

Answer: __________ %

6.  Ebony thinks of a number.  She multiplies it by 3.  She then adds 4.
Her answer is 52.  What was Ebony's original number?

Answer: __________

7.  The graph below shows point P and point Q with a line drawn between them.

Point R is drawn on the line.  It is the same distance from
point P and point Q.  What are the coordinates of point R?

Answer: ( __________ , __________ )

8.    Abed makes a biscuit cutter that looks like shape S.

Abed rotates the cutter 45° clockwise and presses it into
the biscuit dough.  Which shape does he make in the dough?
Circle the correct option.

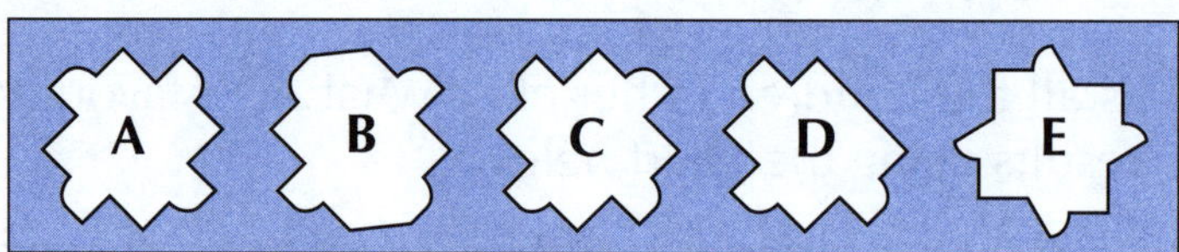


9.    Abigail is buying a bike.  The full price of the bike is £200.
She sees two different offers, as shown below.

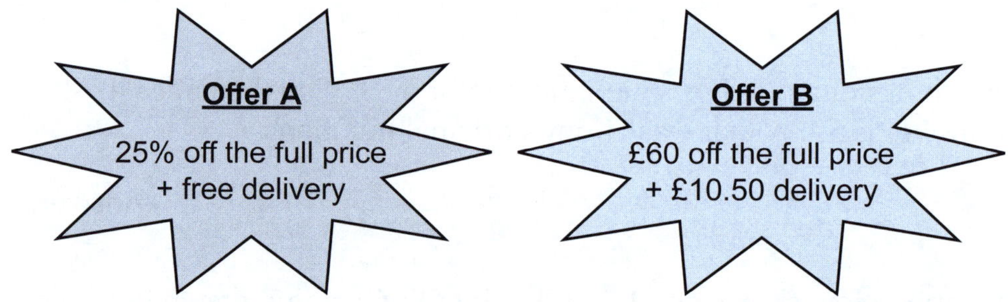


Abigail wants to have her bike delivered.  Which offer is the cheapest?

Answer: Offer ____________

10.   Jaya has ten red candles and eight blue candles.  She lights $^2/_5$ of the red candles
and $^1/_2$ of the blue candles.  How many candles does she light in total?

Answer: ____________

/ 10

You have **10 minutes** to do this test.  Work as quickly and accurately as you can.

1.   Jay rounds the score of his basketball match to the nearest 10.  If he had a rounded score of 60, which of the following could have been his original score?  Circle the correct option.

    **A**   65        **C**   67        **E**   70

    **B**   55        **D**   95

2.   This shape is reflected in the dotted mirror line.

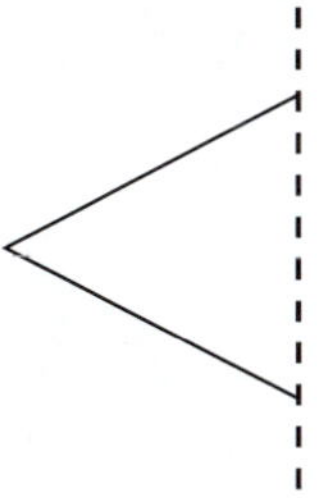

The shape and its reflection together make a new shape.
Circle the name of the new shape.

    **A**   Hexagon        **C**   Triangle        **E**   Rectangle

    **B**   Square        **D**   Parallelogram

3.   Bart is buying some new stationery for school.  He pays with two £10 notes and receives £6.50 in change.  How much did the stationery cost?

Answer: £__________

4.   Gabriella is planting daffodils.  Last year, she planted 32 daffodils and used 2 bags of soil.  This year she wants to plant 96 daffodils.
How many bags of soil will she need?

Answer: __________

5. Rachel creates a sequence using the rule 'multiply the previous number by 2, then add 1 to the result'.  Circle Rachel's sequence from the options below.

**A**   1, 2, 4...
**B**   2, 3, 9...
**C**   2, 5, 11...
**D**   3, 6, 12...
**E**   3, 5, 19...

6. Joel is going to the cinema.  He arrives at the cinema at 16:05, 10 minutes after the film has started.  If the film is two hours long, what time will it finish?  Circle the correct answer.

**A**   17:05
**B**   18:55
**C**   17:35
**D**   18:05
**E**   17:55

7. Michael collects stamps.  He has five red stamps, four green stamps and two blue stamps.  What fraction of his stamps are red?

Answer: __________

8. Kitty is 90 cm tall.  Kitty's older sister Jane is 50% taller.  How tall is Jane?

Answer: __________ cm

9.  The graph below shows the profits of two egg packing companies.

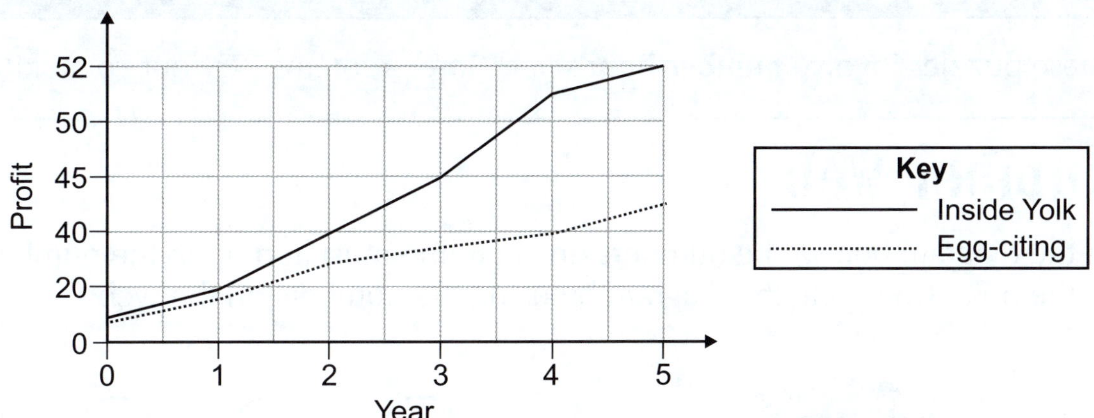


Why is the graph misleading?  Circle the correct statement.

   **A**   Inside Yolk is making too much profit.
   **B**   They only compared themselves against one other company.
   **C**   Some people don't like eggs.
   **D**   The values on the profit axis don't increase evenly.
   **E**   The graph doesn't start at zero.

10.  The diagram below shows a shape made of a square and an equilateral triangle.

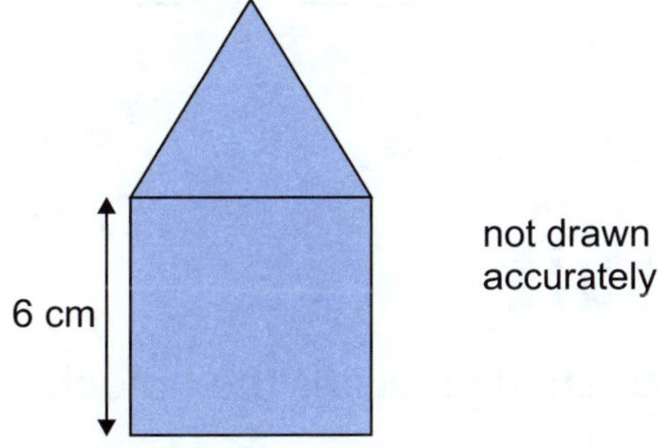


What is the perimeter of the shape?

Answer: __________ cm

/ 10

These puzzles involve **number bonds** and **time** problems.  Try out your skills!

## Number Web

In the diagram below, the numbers on each line must add up to the number in the box.  Complete the diagram by using the numbers on the web.

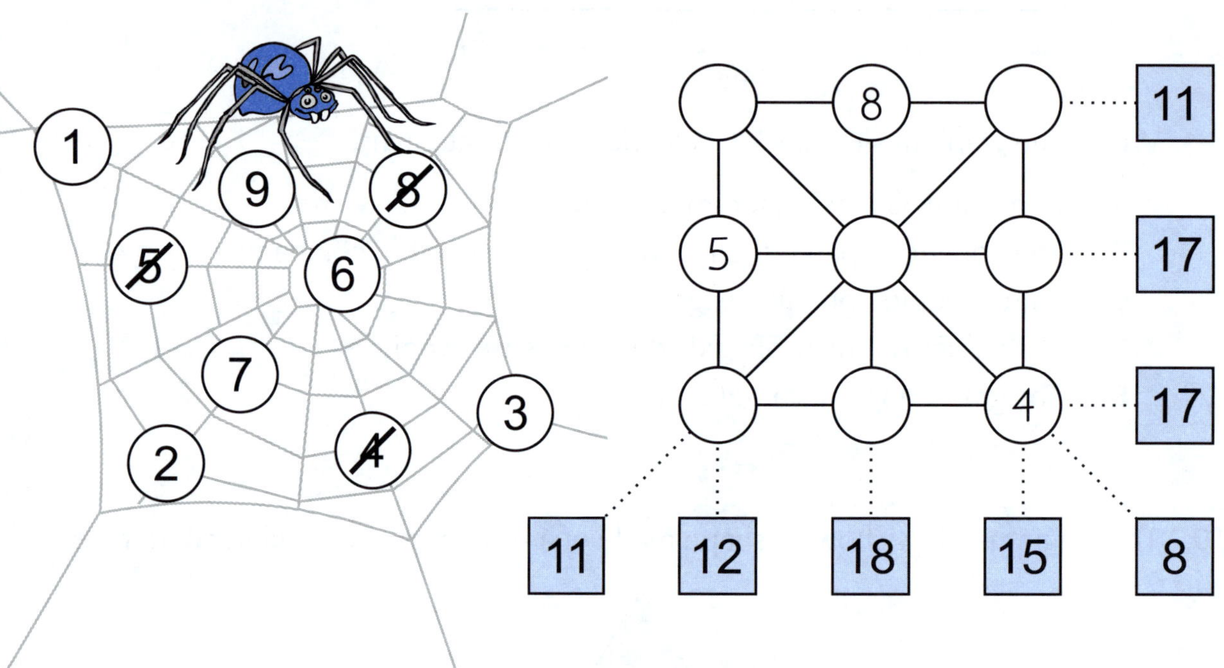

## The Suit Pursuit

Jaspar's suit has been stolen.  He recalls the time that it happened:

- *"It was stolen 30 minutes before I went to the shop."*
- *"I went to the bank 3 hours after I went to the shop."*
- *"I was in the bank for 40 minutes."*
- *"I left the bank at 2:30 pm."*

What time was his suit stolen?

______________ : ______________

You have **10 minutes** to do this test.  Work as quickly and accurately as you can.

1.  What is the correct place value of the underlined digit in 2$\underline{5}$0.47?
    Circle the correct answer.

    **A**  Ones          **C**  Hundreds          **E**  Tenths

    **B**  Tens          **D**  Thousands

2.  Circle the most suitable unit for measuring the deepest part of the ocean.

    **A**  ml          **C**  km          **E**  cm

    **B**  kg          **D**  mm

3.  Kim is practising the shot put.  His last seven throws are found below.

    | 750 cm | 760 cm | 730 cm | 745 cm | 740 cm | 755 cm | 780 cm |

    What is his longest throw in metres?

    Answer: __________ m

4.  Point X on a coordinate grid has coordinates (1, 2).  It moves three squares
    right, and then two squares up.  What are the new coordinates of point X?

    Answer: ( __________ , __________ )

5.  The graph below shows the population of the tiny village of Highstoft.

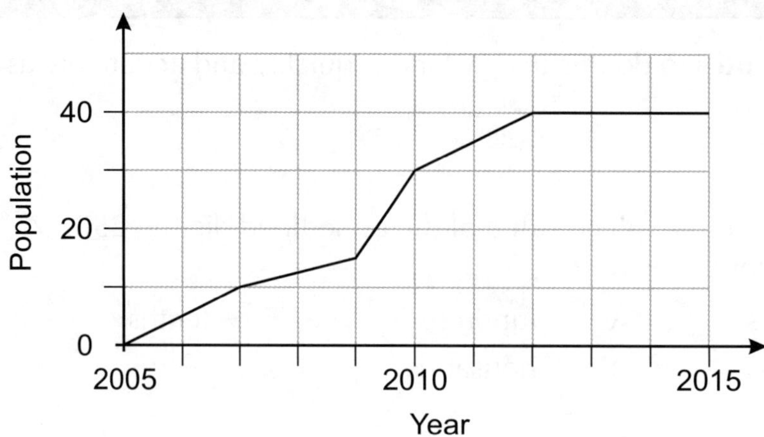

Use the graph to estimate Highstoft's population in 2008.
Circle the correct answer.

| | | | | | |
|---|---|---|---|---|---|
| **A** | 8 people | **C** | 12 people | **E** | 24 people |
| **B** | 18 people | **D** | 10 people | | |

6.  The number of dots on the opposite faces of a fair six-sided dice add up to 7.

How many dots are on the bottom face of the dice above?

Answer: ___________

7.  Anisha thinks of three numbers.  The first two numbers are 8 and 2.
She says, "If I multiply all three numbers together I get 64."
What is Anisha's third number?

Answer: ___________

  

8. A sorting table is given below.  Which number is in the wrong place?
   Circle the correct answer.

|                    | Has a factor of 2 | Has a factor of 3 |
| ------------------ | ----------------- | ----------------- |
| Has a factor of 4  | 16                | 12    36          |
| Has a factor of 5  | 20                | 10                |

**A**   16
**B**   12
**C**   36
**D**   20
**E**   10

9. Terry has 50 pennies.  He gives 20 pennies to his sister.  He then splits
   the remaining pennies into three equal piles and gives one pile to his sister.

   What percentage of Terry's original 50 pennies does his sister now have?

   Answer: __________ %

10. Rudi has a cuboid-shaped rubber, with measurements shown below.

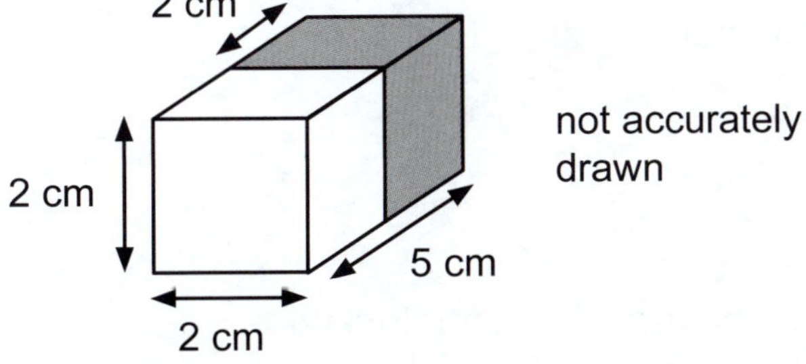


   What is the volume of the white part of his rubber?

   Answer: __________ cm³

/ 10

# Test 27

You have **10 minutes** to do this test.  Work as quickly and accurately as you can.

1.  What fraction of the grid below has been shaded?

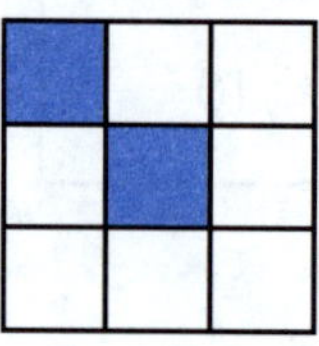

    Answer: ___________

2.  Jenna, Cerys and Shireen were all born on the same day, but in different years.
    Cerys was born in 2004.  Jenna is five years older than Cerys.
    Shireen is two years older than Jenna.

    In what year was Shireen born?

    Answer: ___________

3.  What is the next prime number after 13?

    Answer: ___________

4.  Nora is facing south.  She turns 90° anticlockwise.
    Which direction is she facing now?  Circle the correct answer.

    **A**   North
    **B**   East
    **C**   South
    **D**   West
    **E**   South-East

5.  The number of spots on three different ladybirds are 2, 7 and 10.
    Which of the following statements is true?  Circle the correct option.

   **A**      The total number of spots on all three ladybirds is greater than 20.

   **B**      The total number of spots on all three ladybirds is a multiple of 3.

   **C**      The total number of spots on all three ladybirds is an even number.

   **D**      The total number of spots on all three ladybirds is a square number.

   **E**      None of the above.


6.  A mirror line and point P are shown on the coordinate grid below.

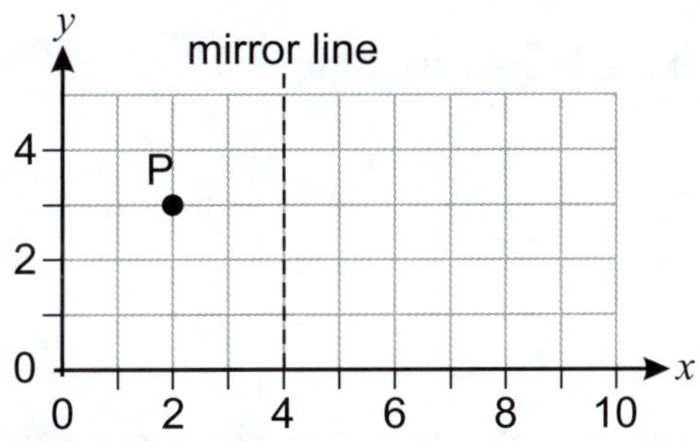


Point P is reflected in the mirror line.  What are the new coordinates of point P?
Circle the correct answer.

   **A**   (4, 5)          **C**   (6, 3)          **E**   (2, 3)

   **B**   (4, 4)          **D**   (6, 4)


7.  A group of 60 adults were asked if they can drive.
    The results are shown in the pie chart below.

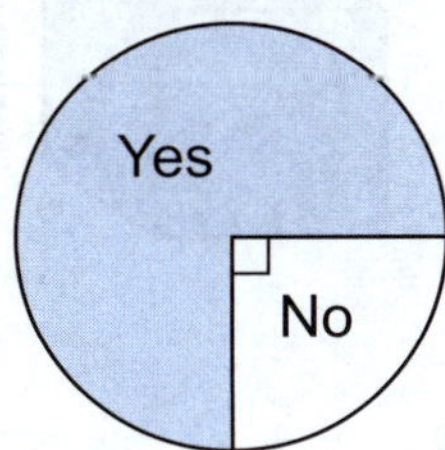


How many adults cannot drive?  Circle the correct answer.

   **A**   0          **C**   30          **E**   45

   **B**   60          **D**   15

8.  The sail on a yacht is made by placing these two right-angled triangles together.
    The lengths of the sides of the bigger triangle are double the lengths of the
    sides of the smaller triangle.

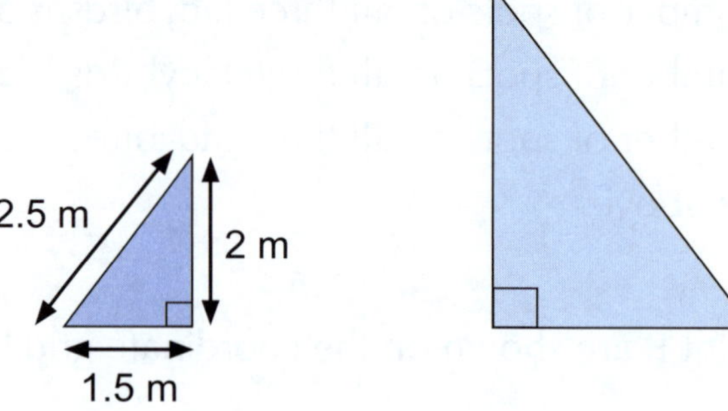


What is the perimeter of the bigger triangle?

Answer: ____________ m

9.  A fountain pours 0.1 litres of water into a basin every minute.
    How many millilitres of water will have been poured into the basin in 12 minutes?

Answer: ____________ ml

10. How would you work out the volume of the cube below?  Circle the correct option.

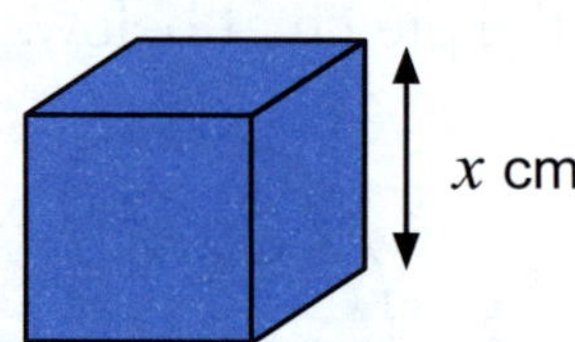


**A**  $x \times x$      **C**  $x + x + x$      **E**  $4 \times x$

**B**  $x \times x \times x$      **D**  $x + x$

/ 10

# Test 28

You have **10 minutes** to do this test.  Work as quickly and accurately as you can.

1.   Which of these fractions is equivalent to $^1/_3$?  Circle the correct option.

    **A**  $^2/_5$        **C**  $^5/_{15}$        **E**  $^4/_9$

    **B**  $^3/_8$        **D**  $^3/_6$

2.   The bill from a restaurant is shown below.

Restaurant bill

Prawn cocktail:  £2.50

Steak & chips:  £4.75

Ice cream:

**Total:**  £10.00

How much did the ice cream cost?

Answer: £ __________

3.   Tilly is thinking of a three-digit number.  She says, "Adding each digit together gives a square number."  Which three-digit number is Tilly thinking of? Circle the correct option.

    **A**  123        **C**  345        **E**  567

    **B**  234        **D**  456

4.   What is $250 \times 12$?

Answer: __________

5.  The bar graph below shows the lengths of four different songs.

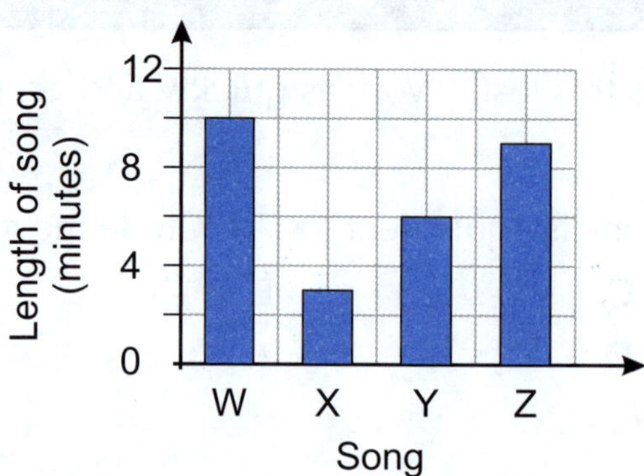



What percentage of the four songs are less than 8 minutes long?

Answer: __________ %

6.  Part of a clock tower in a town square can be seen below.  It is the afternoon.

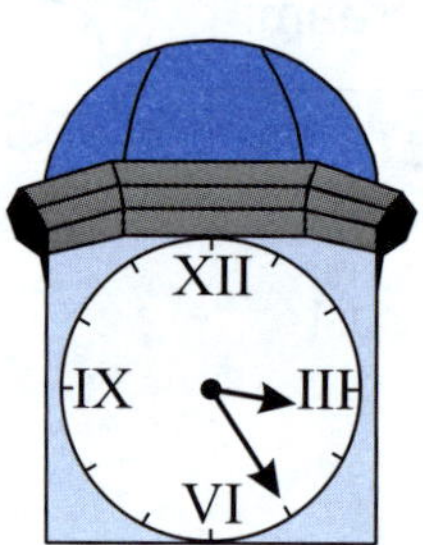



Katie arrived in the town square 1 hour and 20 minutes ago.
What time would it have been then?  Give your answer in 24-hour clock format.

Answer: __________ : __________

7.  Varun's sunflower is 30.4 cm tall.  It grows 2.3 cm each week.
How tall will it be at the end of three weeks?

Answer: __________ cm

8.    Mathedonia has a flag made up of four identical rectangles, as shown below.

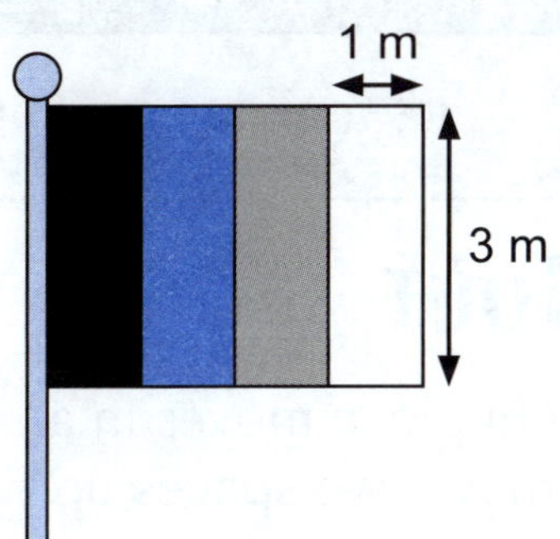



What is the area of the flag?

Answer: __________ m²

9.    Sasha has a collection of blue, grey and white scarves.
      50% of her scarves are blue and 30% are grey.

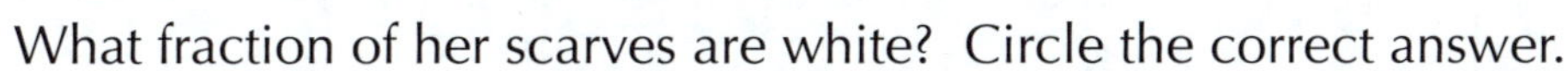

      What fraction of her scarves are white?  Circle the correct answer.

   **A**  $^7/_{10}$        **C**  $^3/_{10}$         **E**  $^1/_2$
   **B**  $^2/_5$           **D**  $^1/_5$

10.  Given that ✚ = 3 and △ = 4, circle the expression below which is not correct.

   **A**  ✚ × △ = 12
   **B**  △ + ✚ = 7
   **C**  ✚ + △ = 7
   **D**  △ + △ = 8
   **E**  ✚ − △ = 1

/ 10

Work through this puzzle — it's a great way to practise using **coordinates**.

# The Knight's Tour

In a game of chess, a knight piece moves in an L-shape.
This means a knight can move two spaces up/down and one space across,
or one space up/down and two spaces across.

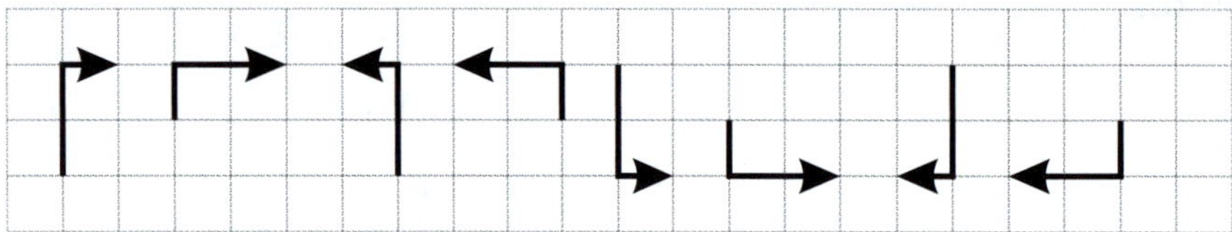

A knight has been placed on the START point on the coordinate grid below.

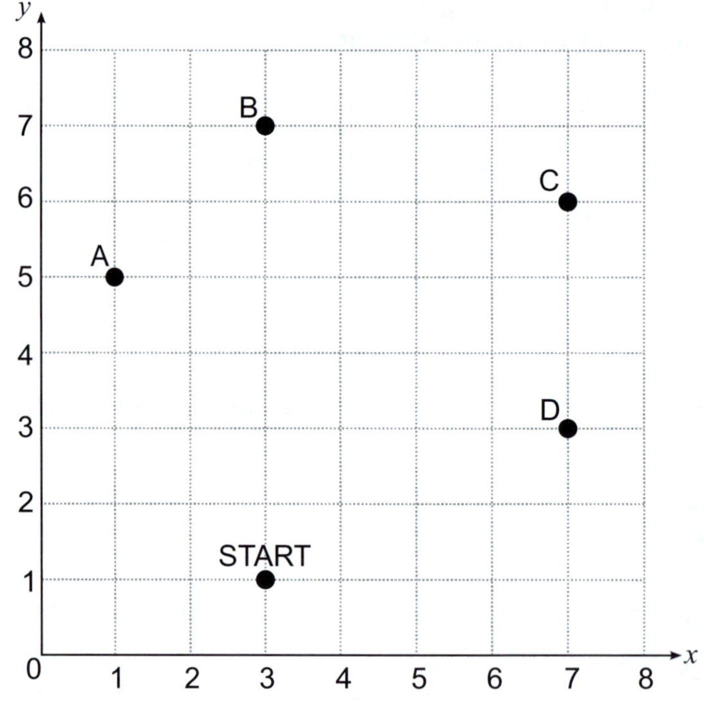

What is the smallest number of moves it will take the
knight to move from START to each point A, B, C and D?

A: _________        B: _________        C: _________        D: _________

# Test 29

You have **10 minutes** to do this test.  Work as quickly and accurately as you can.

1.  Look at the diagram below.  Circle the most sensible estimate of angle *y*.

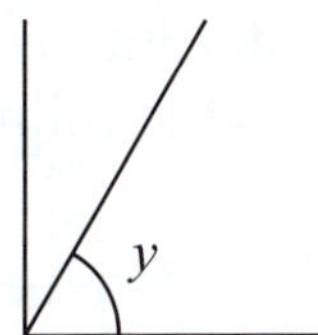

|   |       |   |      |   |       |
|---|-------|---|------|---|-------|
| **A** | 90° | **C** | 30° | **E** | 110° |
| **B** | 45° | **D** | 60° |   |       |

2.  Mary's recipe for 12 brownies uses 200 g of flour.
    How much flour would she need to make 36 brownies?

Answer: _________ g

3.  The colour of every car in a car park is recorded and shown in the pictogram below.

| | |
|---|---|
| Blue |  |
| Black | |
| Red | |
| White | |

**Key**

= 4 cars

Which of the following statements is true?  Circle the correct option.

**A**   There are 28 cars in the car park in total.

**B**   There are four times as many blue cars as black cars.

**C**   White is the most common colour of car in the car park.

**D**   Red is the least common colour of car in the car park.

**E**   There are seven more red cars than white cars.

4. The first five terms in a sequence are 1, 4, 7, 10 and 13.
   What is the seventh term in the sequence?

Answer: __________

5. Rose pours 63.2 ml of blackcurrant squash and 232.4 ml of water into a glass.
   How much liquid does she have in the glass, to the nearest whole millilitre?

Answer: __________ ml

6. Esme has a rectangular piece of patterned material, measuring 8 m by 6 m.
   She cuts a square with sides 3 m long out of the material and throws it away.

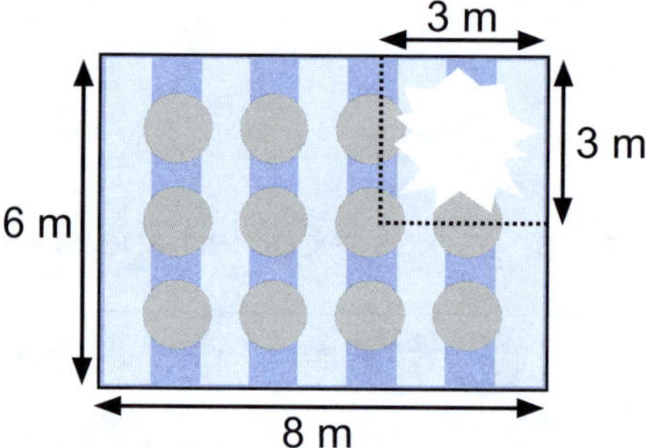


How much material does Esme have left after she cuts out the square?

Answer: __________ m$^2$

7. Elisa has £110 to buy chairs with.  She wants to buy chairs that cost £24 each.
   How many chairs can Elisa buy?

Answer: __________

8.    This incomplete bar chart shows the amount of rainfall in Wetfield each month.
      The amount of rainfall increases by the same amount each month.

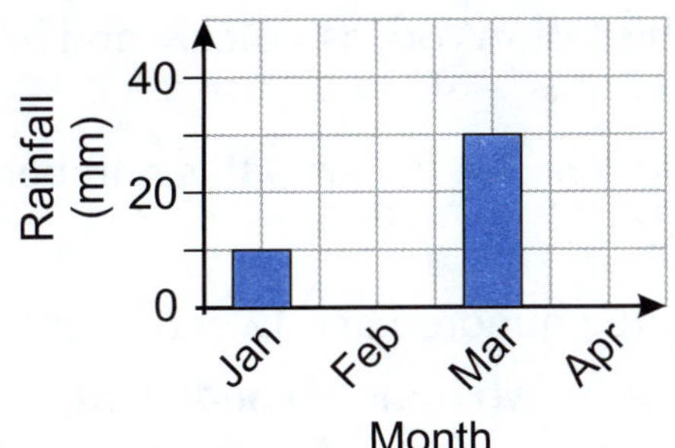


How much rainfall would there be in Wetfield in April?  Circle the correct answer.

**A**    20 mm

**B**    30 mm

**C**    40 mm

**D**    50 mm

**E**    60 mm

9.    Tsu has a pond with fish in his garden.  $\frac{1}{2}$ of the fish are goldfish,
      $\frac{3}{8}$ are koi, and $\frac{1}{8}$ are tench.  There are 6 koi in the pond.
      How many goldfish are in the pond?

Answer: __________

10.   Alex goes on holiday for 10 days.
      She camps for 2 days of the holiday.
      What percentage of the holiday did Alex not camp for?

Answer: __________ %

/ 10

You have **10 minutes** to do this test.  Work as quickly and accurately as you can.

1.  Kai has raised £43 208 for charity.  What is this number in words?
    Circle the correct answer.

    **A**   Four thousand, three hundred and twenty-eight.
    **B**   Forty-three thousand, two hundred and eight.
    **C**   Four hundred and thirty-two thousand, two hundred and eight.
    **D**   Forty-three thousand, two hundred and eighty.
    **E**   Forty-three thousand and twenty-eight.

2.  The shape below is made out of five cubes.

    Circle the view which shows the shape directly from above.

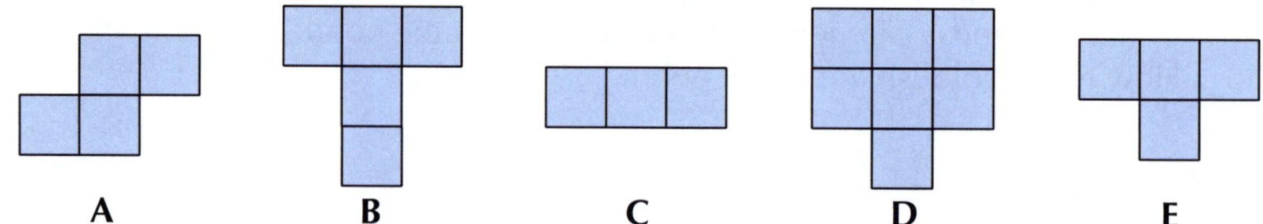

    **A**              **B**              **C**              **D**              **E**

3.  The area of the rectangle below is 54 mm².

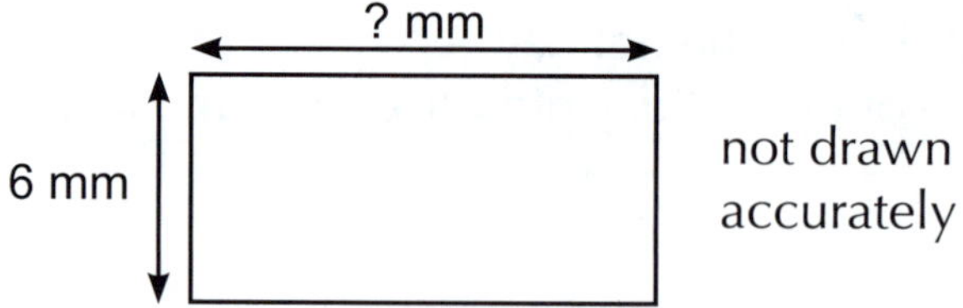

    

    What is the length of the missing side?

    Answer: __________ mm

4.  Mila has 50 DVDs.  28 DVDs are comedies and the rest are action films.
    What percentage of all her DVDs are action films?

Answer: __________ %

5.  Hitesh draws the shape below and cuts it out.  If he folds along the dotted lines,
    what 3D shape will he make?  Circle the correct answer.

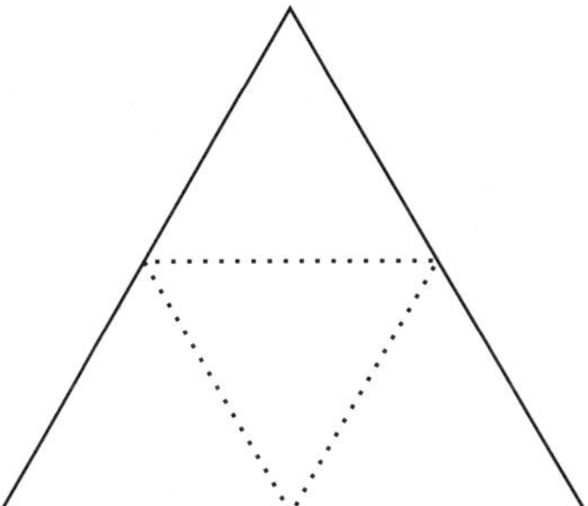

**A**   triangular-based pyramid

**B**   square-based pyramid

**C**   triangular prism

**D**   cone

**E**   cuboid

6.  This incomplete sorting diagram shows the factors of 15 and 27.

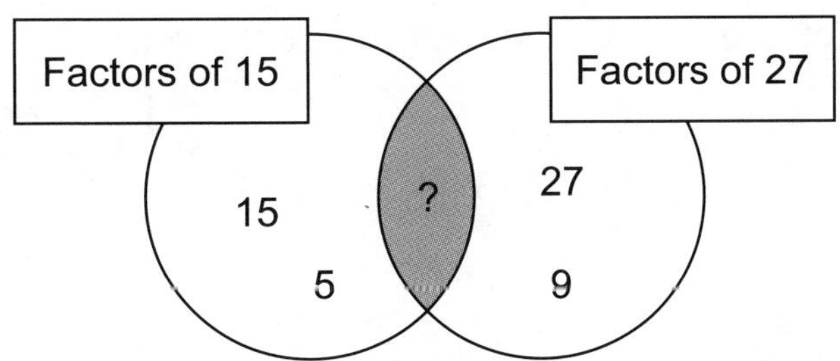


Which of the following numbers can be placed in the shaded area of the diagram?
Circle the correct option.

**A**   6          **C**   4          **E**   7

**B**   3          **D**   2

7.  The first four terms of a sequence are: 4, 1, –2, –5.
    What is the fifth term in the sequence?

Answer: –__________

8.  Francis and Arianna have 36 football stickers between them.
    Arianna has twice as many as Francis.

    How many football stickers does Arianna have?

Answer: __________

9.  Look at the diagram below.

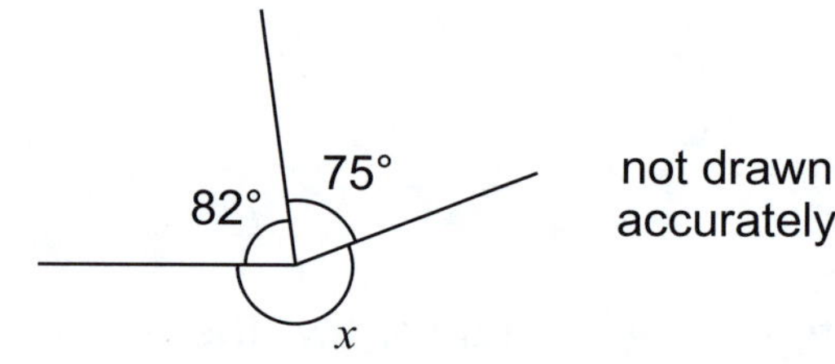


What is the size of angle *x*?  Circle the correct answer.

A   90°          C   78°          E   360°
B   203°         D   193°

10. Andrew runs 2.8 km.  How far is this in centimetres?

Answer: __________ cm

/ 10

    © CGP — not to be photocopied

You have **10 minutes** to do this test.  Work as quickly and accurately as you can.

1.  What number is the arrow pointing to on this ruler?

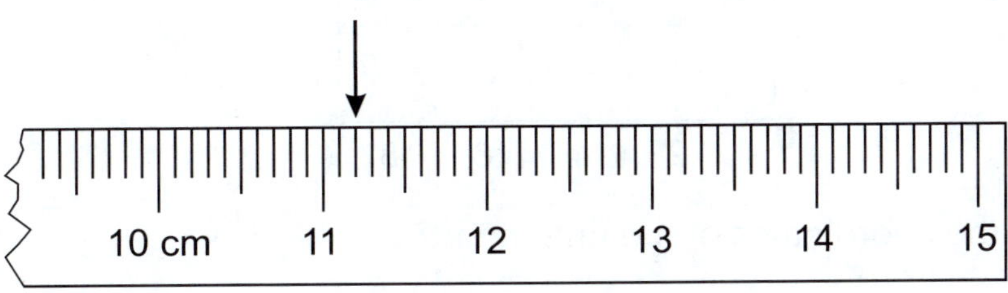

Answer: ___________ cm

2.  Ruth has 10 guinea pigs.  Six of her guinea pigs are short-haired and the rest are long-haired.  What percentage of her guinea pigs are long-haired?

Answer: ___________ %

3.  Cyril started his new job on 4th May.  He got a pay rise exactly three weeks later. On what date did he get his pay rise?  Circle the correct answer.

   **A**   7th May
   **B**   14th May
   **C**   18th May
   **D**   25th May
   **E**   1st June

4.  Monika has $4^2$ books.  Lubo has half as many books as Monika. How many books does Lubo have?

Answer: ___________

      103      

5. Three points of a rectangle have been drawn on a coordinate grid.

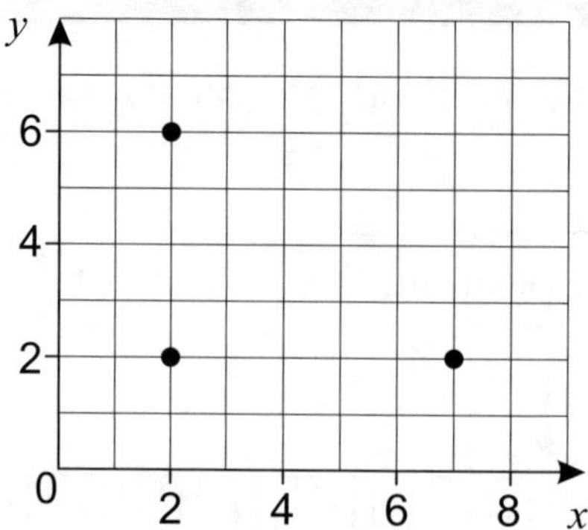

What will be the coordinates of the final point?

Answer: ( ___________ , ___________ )

6. 680 + 680 + 680 + 680 = 340 × ______
Circle the missing number.

   **A**   3

   **B**   4

   **C**   6

   **D**   8

   **E**   16

7. Joseph wins a quiz show.  He gets to open 1 of 5 boxes that contain a cash prize.
Which of the following would give Joseph the largest amount of money?
Circle the correct answer.

   **A**   £1500

   **B**   10% of £10 000

   **C**   $\frac{1}{20}$ of £10 000

   **D**   £100 000 ÷ 100

   **E**   (£5 + £5) × 100

8.  Stu records the temperature in his shed.  His data is shown on the line graph below.

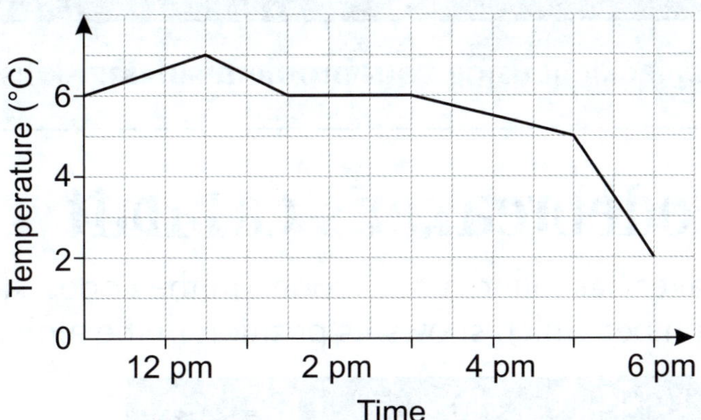

What is the difference between the highest and
lowest temperature that Stu recorded in his shed?

Answer: __________ °C


9.  There are 36 people on a coach.  12 of them are tourists.

What fraction of all the people on the coach aren't tourists?
Circle the correct answer.

**A**  $^1/_4$

**B**  $^1/_2$

**C**  $^2/_5$

**D**  $^1/_3$

**E**  $^2/_3$


10.  What is the value of the ★ in the equation below?

$$(★ × 2) = 32 - 8$$

Answer: __________


/ 10





Test 31

One final puzzle... tackle it using your **problem-solving** skills once again!

# Captain Codebreaker's Calamity

Captain Codebreaker has found a new code.  In the code, each letter is given a number which shows its position in the alphabet.

| A | B | C | D | E | F | G | H | I | J | K | L | M |
|---|---|---|---|---|---|---|---|---|---|---|---|---|
| 1 | 2 | 3 |   |   |   |   |   |   |   |   |   |   |

| N | O | P | Q | R | S | T | U | V | W | X | Y | Z |
|---|---|---|---|---|---|---|---|---|---|---|---|---|
|   |   |   |   |   |   |   |   |   |   |   |   | 26 |

This code can turn numbers into words to uncover secret messages.
Help Captain Codebreaker crack these codes:

> 25, 15, 21    23, 9, 12, 12    14, 5, 22, 5, 18    3, 1, 20, 3, 8    13, 5.

____________________________________________________

> 25, 15, 21    3, 18, 1, 3, 11, 5, 4    20, 8, 5    3, 15, 4, 5.
> 8, 15, 15, 18, 1, 25!

____________________________________________________

____________________________________________________

The total value of a word is found by adding the number of each letter.
Complete the tables below.

| B | E | A | R | Total |
|---|---|---|---|---|
| 2 | 5 | 1 | 18 | **26** |

| C | L | O | U | D | Total |
|---|---|---|---|---|---|
|   |   |   |   |   |   |

| F | O | X | Total |
|---|---|---|---|
|   |   |   |   |

| R | O | C | K | E | T | Total |
|---|---|---|---|---|---|---|
|   |   |   |   |   |   |   |



106

## Test 1 — pages 2-4

**1.   C**
8:15 am to 9:15 am is 60 minutes.
9:15 am to 9:25 am is 10 minutes.
So his total journey is 60 + 10 = 70 minutes.

**2.   48**
Each term is found by multiplying the previous term by 2.
So the next term in the sequence will be 24 × 2 = 48.

**3.   30 m**
The garden is a rectangle, so it must have two sides of
10 m and two sides of 5 m.
5 + 10 + 5 + 10 = 30 m.

**4.   C**
39 can be divided by 1, 3, 13 and 39,
so it is not a prime number.

**5.   84**
Work out the brackets first.
(54 − 42) × 7 = 12 × 7 = 84.

**6.   6**
Laura has 11 green sweets and 5 red sweets.
11 − 5 = 6 sweets.

**7.   E**
A is false because 30 is not a multiple of 4.
B is false because 16 is not a multiple of 5.
C is false because 25 is not a multiple of 4.
D is false because 24 is not a multiple of 5.
E is correct because 40 is a multiple of 4 and 5.

**8.   38 km**
Partition 13.5 into 13 and 0.5 before adding them to
24.7.  24.7 + 13 = 37.7 km.
37.7 + 0.5 = 38.2 km.
To round 38.2 km to the nearest whole kilometre, round
the digit in the ones column.  8 is being rounded, and 2 is
less than 5, so 38.2 km rounds down to 38 km.

**9.   40%**
20 − 12 = 8, so Abdul eats 8 cakes out of the
20 cakes.  $^{8}/_{20}$ = $^{40}/_{100}$ = 40%.

**10.   C**
1 flowerpot needs 300 g of clay, so 10 flowerpots need
10 × 300 g = 3000 g of clay.  30 = 3 × 10,
so 30 flowerpots need 3 × 3000 g = 9000 g of clay.
1 kg = 1000 g, so 9000 g = 9 kg.

## Test 2 — pages 5-7

**1.   D**
Putting the jumps in order of length gives:
2.7 m, 3 m, 3.5 m, 4 m, 4.3 m.  So the longest jump was
4.3 m on Thursday.

**2.   D**
The 3 in 123 540 is in the thousands column, which is
the furthest to the left of the decimal point.

**3.   18°**
The angles in a triangle add up to 180°.
So $x$ = 180° − 90° − 72° = 18°.

**4.   (3, 4)**
Point T is at (8, 7).  Moving 5 squares left gives an
$x$-coordinate of 3.  Moving 3 squares down gives a
$y$-coordinate of 4.

**5.   21:05**
Adding 1 hour and 40 minutes to 7pm takes it to
8:40pm.  You can then add in the interval, which
is 25 minutes.  Split the interval into 20 minutes
and 5 minutes.  Adding the 20 minutes takes it to
9pm, and adding the 5 minutes takes it to 9:05pm.
Add 12 hours to turn it into 24-hour clock format:
9:05 + 12 = 21:05.

**6.   40 cm**
Find the three missing lengths.

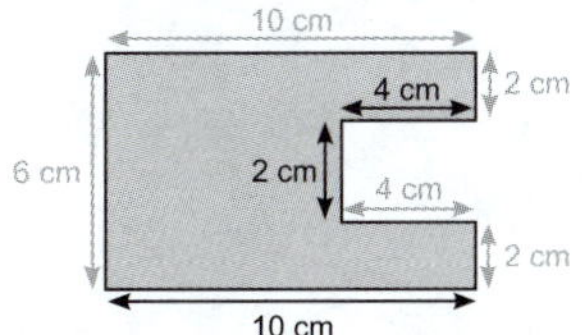


Now add all the lengths of the sides together:
10 + 2 + 4 + 2 + 4 + 2 + 10 + 6 = 40 cm.

**7.   A**
Turn all the numbers into percentages.  $^{3}/_{5}$ = 60%,
0.25 = 25%, $^{1}/_{10}$ = 10%.  So $^{3}/_{5}$ is the biggest.

**8.   24**
Diego wants to make 12 ÷ 3 = 4 times more omelettes.
So he will need 6 × 4 = 24 eggs.

**9.   C**
After 40 minutes Nadine has completed half of her
journey.  So the full length of her journey will be
40 × 2 = 80 minutes.  1 hour = 60 minutes,
so 80 minutes = 1 hour 20 minutes.

**10.   B**
7 red + 6 blue + 2 white = 15 t-shirts are not green.
18 − 15 = 3 green t-shirts.
Ed has 18 t-shirts in total, so $^{1}/_{6}$ are green.

# Test 3 — pages 8-10

**1.     56 800**
To round 56 782 to the nearest hundred,
you need to round the digit in the hundreds column.
7 is being rounded.  8 is greater than 5,
so 56 782 rounds up to 56 800.

**2.     5**
Each symbol on the pictogram shows 2 ice creams.
So each $^1/_2$ symbol shows 1 ice cream.
Becky sold 5 $^1/_2$ symbols of vanilla
$= 5 \times 2 + 1 = 11$ vanilla ice creams.
She also sold 3 symbols of strawberry =
$3 \times 2 = 6$ strawberry ice creams.  $11 - 6 = 5$, so she sold
5 more vanilla ice creams than strawberry ice creams.

**3.     108°**
Angles around a point add up to 360°.
So angle $x = 360° - 252° = 108°$.

**4.     6**
1 litre = 1000 ml, so 2 litres = 2000 ml.
The number of glasses that can be filled is $2000 \div 300$.
Divide both numbers by 100 first to simplify them.
$2000 \div 100 = 20, 300 \div 100 = 3$.
So $20 \div 3 = $  $\begin{array}{r} 6 \ \ r2 \\ 3\overline{)20} \end{array}$

So 6 whole glasses can be filled.

**5.     B**
The volume of a cuboid is length × width × height.
So $5 \times 2 \times 3 = 30$ cm$^3$.

**6.     5.0**
The next term in the sequence is found by adding 0.5
to the previous term.  So $4.5 + 0.5 = 5.0$.

**7.     E**

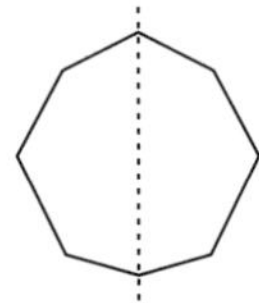

The new shape has 8 sides, so must be an octagon.

**8.     40 °C**

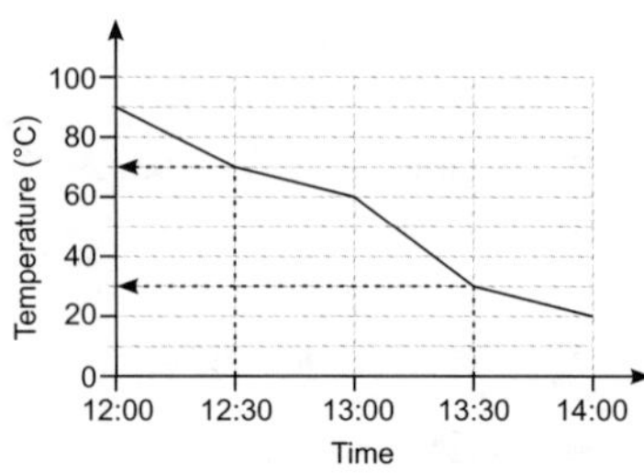

The temperature at 12:30 is 70 °C.
The temperature at 13:30 is 30 °C.
$70 - 30 = 40$ °C.

**9.     B**
A is false because $5 + 9 + 7 = 21$ (odd).
C is false because $3 + 11 + 11 = 25$ (odd).
D is false because $2 + 5 + 8 = 15$ (odd).
E is false because $23 + 25 + 21 = 69$ (odd).
B is correct because $15 + 6 + 13 = 34$ (even).

**10.     E**
Carmen has $10 - 7 = 3$ white marbles.  When she takes
one black marble out of the bag, there will be 9 marbles
in total left.  6 will be black and 3 will be white.  So the
fraction of white marbles left in the bag will be $^3/_9 = {}^1/_3$.

# Puzzles 1 — page 11

### The Postman's Factor Path
The factors of 24 are 1, 2, 3, 4, 6, 8, 12 and 24.
So Percy's path is:

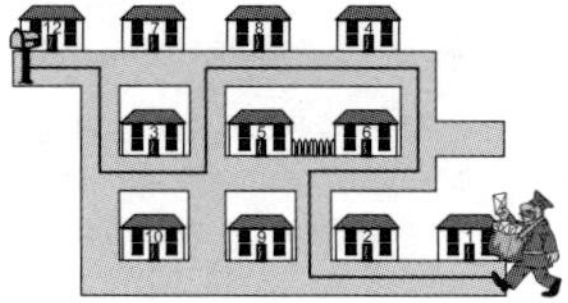

### Domino Dilemma
When lined up in order, 56 is in the middle, so the order
could be:  50, 54, 56, 57, ? / 50, 54, 56, ?, 57 or
50, 54, ?, 56, 57.  The difference between the lowest and
highest score is 10, which rules out the second and third
options $(57 - 50 = 7)$.
$? - 50 = 10$, so the missing score is 60.

# Test 4 — pages 12-14

**1.     C**
Acute angles are less than 90° and obtuse angles are
greater than 90°. Options A, B and D are false because
they have 1 obtuse angle.  Option E is false because it
has a right angle.

**2.     26°**
The difference between −6 °C and 0 °C is 6 °C.
The difference between 0 °C and 20 °C is 20 °C.
So the difference between −6 °C and 20 °C is
$6 + 20 = 26$ °C.

**3.     30**
There are 60 minutes in an hour.  $60 \div 10 = 6$,
so Bonnie could read $5 \times 6 = 30$ pages in an hour.

**4.     C**
A is false because 3 is not a factor of 28.
B is false because 5 is not a factor of 28.
D is false because 3 and 5 are not factors of 28.
E is false because 3 is not a factor of 28.
C is correct because 2 and 7 are factors of 28.

**5.    8 cm²**
Add up the number of shaded squares on the grid.
Each square has an area of 1 cm².
There are 8 shaded squares, so the area of
the shaded shape is 8 × 1 cm² = 8 cm².

**6.    A**
0.7 + 0.2 = 0.9.  0.9 = $^9/_{10}$.

**7.    D**
Thursday is the first day when the potato line is higher on
the graph than the carrot line.

**8.    36 cm**
50% of 12 = 12 ÷ 2 = 6.  So the width of the
rectangle is 6 cm.  The perimeter of the rectangle is
12 + 6 + 12 + 6 = 36 cm.

**9.    E**
The distance of 3 forest laps is 3 × 3 = 9 km.
The distance of 5 garden laps is 5 × 0.5 = 2.5 km.
So the total distance is 9 + 2.5 = 11.5 km.

**10.    £15.60**
2 metres of fabric cost 2 × £5.60 = £11.20.
4 buttons cost 4 × £1.10 = £4.40.
So Bill's total cost is £11.20 + £4.40 = £15.60.

# Test 5 — pages 15-17
**1.    15 cm²**
13 squares have been fully shaded.  Two squares are
shaded over 50% and two squares are shaded less
than 50%.  Adding these four squares together will give
approximately 2 squares.

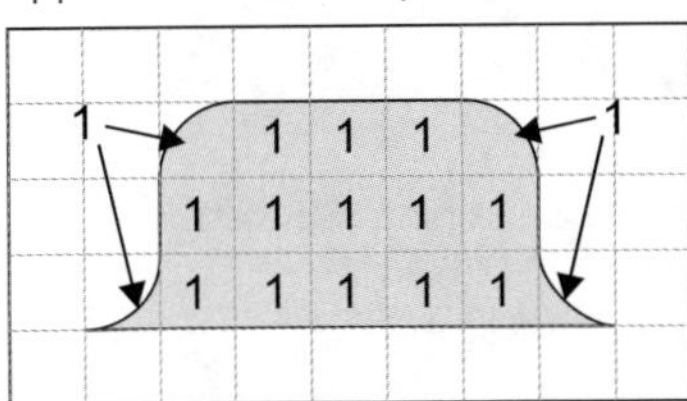

13 + 2 = 15, so the area is approximately 15 cm².

**2.    80°**
Angles in a triangle add up to 180°.  So the size of the
missing angle = 180° − 50° − 50° = 80°.

**3.    B**
The total number of animals she owns is 2 + 3 + 5 = 10.
5 of those are chickens, so the fraction of animals that
are chickens is $^5/_{10} = ^1/_2$.

**4.    30 cm**
Putting the wood in order gives:  19 cm, 25 cm, 30 cm,
35 cm, 42 cm.  The middle value is 30 cm.

**5.    4**
1 kg = 1000 g, so 1.6 kg = 1600 g.  If 1 bag of flour =
500 g, 3 bags of flour = 500 × 3 = 1500 g, which isn't
enough.  500 × 4 = 2000 g, which is enough, so you
would need to buy 4 bags of flour.

**6.    C**
42 is double 21, so 4830 × 42 will be double
4830 × 21.  4830 × 42 = 101 430 × 2 = 202 860.

**7.    8**
20% = $^1/_5$.  So 20% of 40 = $^1/_5$ of 40 = 40 ÷ 5 = 8.

**8.    A**
Marcus has 3 more apps than John, so John has
3 fewer apps than Marcus.  Marcus has ★ apps,
so John has ★ − 3 apps.

**9.    13.5 m**
1 m = 100 cm, so 350 cm = 3.5 m.
10 + 3.5 = 13.5 m.

**10.    (4, 7)**
Point P is 3 squares away from the mirror line, so its
reflection will also be 3 squares away from it, but on the
other side of the line.  This is (4, 7).

# Puzzles 2 — page 18
## Market Maths Mayhem
🍞 − 🍎 = 30p: 50p − 🍎 = 30p. So 🍎 = 20p.

🥕 − 🍎 = 🍎: 🥕 − 20p = 20p. So 🥕 = 40p.

🍎 + 🥕 = 🍊: 20p + 40p = 🍊. So 🍊 = 60p.

## The Sweet Thief
The person who stole the sweets is Alfred.

# Test 6 — pages 19-21
**1.    $^3/_5$**
There are 3 regular polygons out of a total of
5 shapes.  As a fraction, this is $^3/_5$.

**2.    £6**
Amjad makes 50p − 10p = 40p profit
on each chocolate bar.  He sells 15 chocolate bars,
so partition 15 into 10 + 5.
Then multiply 40p by each of these parts:
10 × 40p = 400p, 5 × 40p = 200p,
400p + 200p = 600p = £6.

**3.    C**
A is false because Sharon made the most cards on
Sunday.  B is false because Sharon made a total of
28 + 36 = 64 cards on Saturday and Sunday.
D is false because Sharon made the fewest number of
cards on Monday and Thursday.
E is false because Sharon made 30 − 18
= 12 more cards on Tuesday than Thursday.
C is correct because 18, 30, 24, 22, 28 and 36 are all
even numbers.

**4.    35**
Each term is found by adding 4 to the previous term.
So the fifth term in the sequence will be 35.





Answers

**5.   5**
$^1/_2$ of a toast icon represents $2 \div 2 = 1$ person,
so $2 + 2 + 1 = 5$ people prefer butter.
$2 + 2 + 2 + 2 + 2 = 10$ people prefer chocolate spread,
so $10 - 5 = 5$ people prefer chocolate spread to butter.

**6.   £85**
Partition 17 into $10 + 7$ and multiply 5 by
each of these parts:  $10 \times £5 = £50$, $7 \times £5 = £35$,
$£50 + £35 = £85$.

**7.   A**
There are $4 + 2 + 3 + 1 = 10$ vegetables in total.
So there are 4 carrots out of 10 vegetables.
As a fraction, this is $^4/_{10}$.  $^4/_{10} = {}^{40}/_{100} = 40\%$.

**8.   D**
Half a turn is 180°.  Leeroy turns another 90°,
so he has turned $180° + 90° = 270°$ clockwise in total.

**9.   11 cm**
The area of the mirror is given by $? \times 6 = 66$ cm$^2$.
So, $? = 66 \div 6 = 11$ cm.

**10.   225 ml**
$^1/_4$ of $600 = 600 \div 4 = 150$ ml.
So $600 - 150 = 450$ ml left.
$^1/_2$ of $450 = 450 \div 2 = 225$ ml.
So there is 225 ml of orange juice left.

## Test 7 — pages 22-24

**1.   4**
3 boxes hold $3 \times 6 = 18$ pieces of scampi.
4 boxes hold $4 \times 6 = 24$ pieces of scampi.
So Tuscany should buy 4 boxes of scampi.

**2.   A**

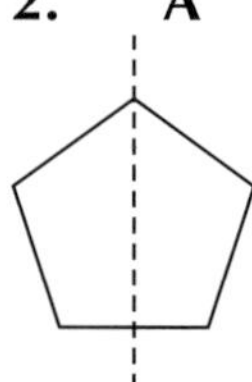

The new shape has 5 sides, so must be a pentagon.

**3.   B**

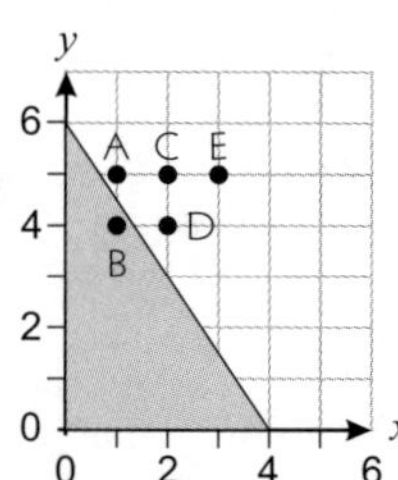

Plotting each point on the coordinate grid shows that
only B is inside the triangle.

**4.   65**
In Year 5, Cole scored 25 in Maths, 15 in English
and 25 in Science.  So his total score for Year 5 was
$25 + 15 + 25 = 65$.

**5.   £4.25**
Divide £12.75 by 3.
$£12 \div 3 = £4$ and $£0.75 \div 3 = £0.25$,
so $£12.75 \div 3 = £4 + £0.25 = £4.25$.

**6.   54 minutes**
$10\%$ of $60 = 60 \div 10 = 6$ minutes.
$60 - 6 = 54$ minutes.

**7.   64**
There are two boxes with 20 toys in, which gives Dean
$2 \times 20 = 40$ toys.  There are three boxes with 10 toys,
which gives Dean $3 \times 10 = 30$ toys.
So in total, Dean has $30 + 40 = 70$ toys.
$8^2 = 8 \times 8 = 64$, and $9^2 = 9 \times 9 = 81$, so 64 is the
closest square number to 70.

**8.   B**
10 000 kg is far too heavy for a pencil, computer,
dog and tiger.  So the most likely answer is a bus.

**9.   10**
Each term is found by adding 7 to the previous term.
So the missing first term in the sequence will be
$17 - 7 = 10$.

**10.   7**
To get 290 points in the fewest number of stones,
add $100 + 100 + 20 + 20 + 20 + 20 + 10$.
This is 7 different stones.

## Test 8 — pages 25-27

**1.   18 cm³**
The cuboid has 2 layers, each containing 9 cubes.
So there are $2 \times 9 = 18$ cubes in total.
Each cube is 1 cm$^3$, so the volume is 18 cm$^3$.

**2.   C**
Length is a distance, so it can't be m$^2$
(which measures area), or kg (which measures mass).
km are too big to measure the length of a
car sensibly and cm are too small to measure the
length of a car sensibly.  A car is usually several
metres long, so the most sensible unit is m.

**3.   60 cm**
A regular pentagon has 5 sides of the same length.
Each side is 12 cm, so the perimeter is $5 \times 12 = 60$ cm.

**4.   D**
1 hour = 60 minutes, so 1 hour and 20 minutes
$= 60 + 20 = 80$ minutes.
Sarah takes 50 minutes on the way back,
so her total journey is $80 + 50 = 130$ minutes.

**5.   27°**
There are 180° along a straight line.
So angle $x = 180° - 153° = 27°$.

## 6. £18

Read off the graph at months 6 and 2:

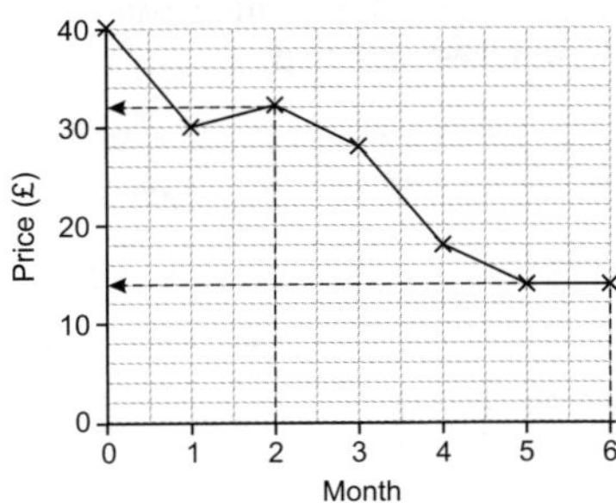

Month 2 is £32 and month 6 is £14.
So the difference is £32 − £14 = £18.

## 7. 27

You know that ♥ ÷ 3 = 4 + 5 = 9, so ♥ is a number that gives 9 when it is divided by 3.
So ♥ must be 27.

## 8. B

4 is being rounded. The 5 in the hundredths column means the 4 rounds up, giving 678.5.

## 9. 94

C = 100, X = 10, V = 5, I = 1.
Small numerals before big ones are subtracted,
so XC is C − X = 90 and IV = V − I = 4.
So XCIV = 90 + 4 = 94.

## 10. E

A is false because if they both had at least 6 pencils, they would have at least 6 + 6 = 12 pencils in total.
B is false because half of 11 is 5.5, which isn't a whole number of pencils.
C is false because adding two even numbers always gives an even number.
D is false because if Gerald has 3 pencils, and Hashim has 3 × 3 = 9 pencils, the total number of pencils would be 3 + 9 = 12 pencils.
E is correct because Hashim could have 7 pencils, Gerald could have 4 pencils and 7 + 4 = 11.

# Puzzles 3 — page 28

## Primes and Ca-nines

Cross off all multiples of 9 on their teeth:
9, 27, 63 and 99.
Cross off prime numbers greater than 9 on their teeth:
11, 13, 17 and 19.
Bill will have the fewest teeth left, and will have 2 fewer than Ben.

## Where Goes the Hare?

Sequence 1: 7
Sequence 2: 11

# Test 9 — pages 29-31

## 1. C

A is false because the time between Hopford and Jumpville is 55 minutes. B is false because the time between Hopford and Skipmouth is 2 hours and 10 minutes. D is false because the time between Jumpville and Leapfield is 2 hours.
E is false because the time between Hopford and Leapfield is 2 hours and 55 minutes.

## 2. D

A right angle is 90° and angle $x$ is greater than a right angle, which rules out options A, C and E.
A straight line is 180° and angle $x$ is less than a straight line, which rules out option B.

## 3. 3 years

1 m = 100 cm, so the earthworm grows 0.02 m = 2 cm a year. Growing 8 − 2 = 6 cm in total, will take 6 ÷ 2 = 3 years.

## 4. 7 cm³

Each cube is 1 cm³.
There are 7 blocks, so the total volume is 7 cm³.

## 5. C

Reading off the graph, only one child's name begins with J. There are 30 children in total, so the fraction of children's names that begin with the letter J is $^1/_{30}$.

## 6. 1400

To round 1352 to the nearest 100, round the digit in the hundreds column. 3 is being rounded, and the 5 in the tens column means it's being rounded up, so 1352 rounds up to 1400.

## 7. XVI

X = 10, V = 5, I = 1.
Small numerals after big numerals are added on,
so XV is 15 and XVI = XV + I = 16.

## 8. 10

The number of triangles in each term is 1, 3, 6...
So first add 2, then 3 and so on.
So the next term will be 6 + 4 = 10.

## 9. 270 g

For 9 grandchildren, Doris will need 3 times as much flour.
90 × 3 = 270 g.

## 10. 5 hours

The difference between temperatures is 18 − 8 = 10 °C.
Every hour, the temperature increases by 2 °C,
so 10 ÷ 2 = 5 hours.

# Test 10 — pages 32-34

**1.    12 cm**
An equilateral triangle has 3 sides of the same length.
Each side is 4 cm, so the perimeter is 4 × 3 = 12 cm.

**2.    9.7 g**
There are 10 divisions between 9 g and 10 g, so each
division is worth 1 ÷ 10 = 0.1 g.  The arrow is pointing to
7 divisions after 9 g, so it is pointing to 9.7 g.

**3.    4.6 m**
Use the column method for multiplication to work out the
height of the giraffe in cm (115 × 4):

$$\begin{array}{r} 115 \\ \times \quad 4 \\ \hline 460 \\ {}_{2} \end{array}$$

So the giraffe is 460 cm tall.  100 cm = 1 m,
so this is 4.6 m.

**4.    D**
$1/7 + 2/7 = 3/7$ of the sweets are either blue or green.
$1 - 3/7 = 4/7$ of the sweets are yellow.

**5.    C**
B and D are false because Rhiannon is describing a
three-sided shape, which makes it a triangle.
A is false because  the angles are all equal
in an equilateral triangle.
E is false because two of the angles in an isosceles
triangle must be the same.

**6.    6**
5 people exercised for 2 hours and 1 person exercised for
3 hours.  So the total number of people who exercised for
2 or more hours is 5 + 1 = 6 people.

**7.    £37.50**
Hiring a black suit for 7 hours costs £12.50 × 7.
Partition £12.50 into £12 and £0.50
and multiply 7 by each of these parts:
£12 × 7 = £84, £0.50 × 7
= £3.50, £84 + £3.50 = £87.50.
A white suit costs £50 to hire for the day,
so is £87.50 – £50 = £37.50 cheaper.

**8.    $30**
Read off the graph at £20:

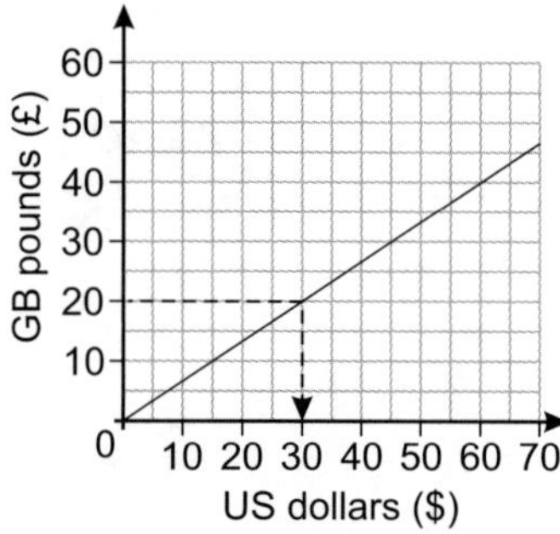


She gets $30.

**9.    C**
The denominators are the same, so do 4 − 1 + 3 = 6 to
get $6/5$.  Turn it into a mixed number: 5 goes into 6 with
remainder 1, so $6/5 = 1\,1/5$, which is option C.

**10.    110**
(5 + 6) × 10 = 11 × 10 = 110.

# Puzzles 4 — page 35

**Parcel Panic**
Half of 16 is 8, which rules out box 9.
Multiples of 3 are 3 and 6, which rules out box 4.
Prime numbers are 2, 3, 5, 7, 11.
6 is one less than 7, so Jerry's box is box 6.

**Bizarre Biscuits**

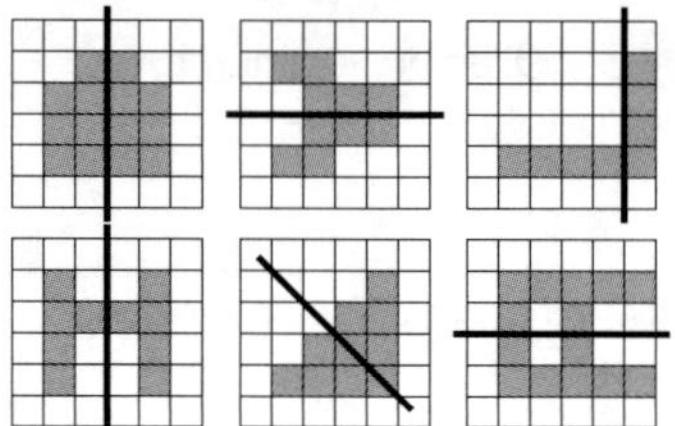

# Test 11 — pages 36-38

**1.    1.3**
There are 10 divisions between 1 and 2, so each
division is worth 1 ÷ 10 = 0.1.  The arrow is pointing
to 3 divisions after 1, so it is pointing to 1.3.

**2.    C**
An obtuse angle is between 90° and 180° and the angle
is roughly 150°, so option C is correct.

**3.    (9, 4)**
Moving four squares east (right) gives an $x$-coordinate of
9.  Moving three squares north (up) gives a $y$-coordinate
of 4, so the treasure is moved to (9, 4).

**4.    C**
A is false because it has five lines of symmetry.
B is false because it has infinitely many lines of symmetry.
D is false because it has four lines of symmetry.
E is false because it has six lines of symmetry.

**5.    D**
1 kg = 1000 g, so A is 1800 g and C is 1960 g.
D is 1974 g, so the heaviest rabbit is D.

**6.    20 m²**
Each square is 1 m² and there are 20 squares that make
up the pond, so the area is 1 m² × 20 = 20 m².

**7.    C**
In total there are 35 + 30 + 15 + 20 = 100 pages.
So $30/100 = 3/10$ of the pages are about dragons.

**8. 10**

Reading off the graph, 12 people said they prefer summer and 2 people said they prefer winter.
So 12 – 2 = 10 people prefer summer to winter.

**9. E**

Basil buys 3 apples and 3 bananas in total (3A + 3B).
A is false because this expression is for buying three apples and one banana.
B is false because you can't multiply an apple and a banana together.
C is false because this expression is for buying one apple and one banana.
D is false because this expression is for buying one apple and three bananas.
E is correct because $3 \times (A + B) = 3A + 3B$ and this expression is for buying three apples and three bananas.

**10. £6.48**

$3 \times £1.50 = £4.50$ and $2 \times 99p = £1.98$.
So in total she spends £4.50 + £1.98 = £6.48.
(Use partitioning or the column method.)

# Test 12 — pages 39-41

**1. A**

The shortest height is 1.23 m, which is A.

**2. 7**

6 containers hold $6 \times 300 = 1800$ g and
7 containers hold $7 \times 300 = 2100$ g,
so she would need 7 containers.

**3. B**

5300 g is 100 times larger than 53 g.
So multiply £2.66 by 100 by moving the decimal point two places to the right to get £266.00

**4. 24**

4 box sets cost $4 \times £12 = £48$.
5 box sets cost $5 \times £12 = £60$.
So she can only buy 4 box sets with £50.
Each box set contains 6 DVDs, so she can get $6 \times 4 = 24$ DVDs in total.

**5. C**

10% of 400 g = 400 g ÷ 10 = 40 g.
So 10% more is 400 g + 40 g = 440 g.

**6. B**

In total there are 9 whole circles and one half circle.
So $(9 \times 2) + 1 = 19$ hats were sold in total.
Baseball caps has 3 whole circles, so $3 \times 2 = 6$ baseball caps were sold. This as a fraction of all hats sold is $^{6}/_{19}$.

**7. 19:23**

1 hour = 60 minutes, so 3 hours = 180 minutes.
173 minutes is 7 minutes away from 180 minutes.
So 180 minutes from 16:30 is 19:30, and subtracting 7 minutes means Chris arrived at 19:23.

**8. 27 cm³**

The volume of the cube is height × length × width, which is $3 \times 3 \times 3 = 27$ cm³.

**9. 15**

Each term in the sequence has one extra row with one more dot than the previous term.
The fourth term would have 6 + 4 = 10 dots and the fifth term would have 10 + 5 = 15 dots.

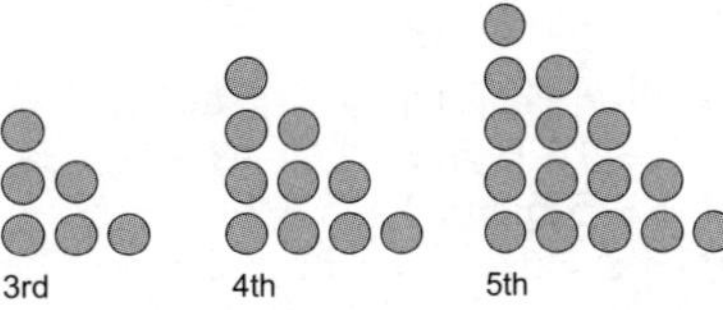


**10. 17.6 m**

An octagon has 8 sides, so the perimeter is $8 \times 2.2$ m.
Partition 2.2 into 2 and 0.2 and multiply each part separately: $8 \times 2 = 16$, $8 \times 0.2 = 1.6$,
16 + 1.6 = 17.6 m.

# Test 13 — pages 42-44

**1. A**

Australia is the largest sector, so the answer is A.

**2. D**

A cake costs 16p more than a salad, so option D is false.

**3. 9**

8 minibuses hold $8 \times 9 = 72$ people, which is too few.
9 minibuses hold $9 \times 9 = 81$ people, which is enough.
So 9 minibuses would be needed.

**4. B**

1 kg = 1000 g. So 1.8 kg = 1800 g.
1800 – 300 = 1500 g = 1.5 kg.

**5. A**

15 is not a factor of 24 and should be in the odd numbers section of the sorting diagram.

**6. £48**

20% of £40 = £40 ÷ 5 = £8.
So the new ticket price is £40 + £8 = £48.

**7. 98°**

Angles around a point add up to 360°.
So angle $x = 360° – 188° – 74° = 98°$.

**8. 2**

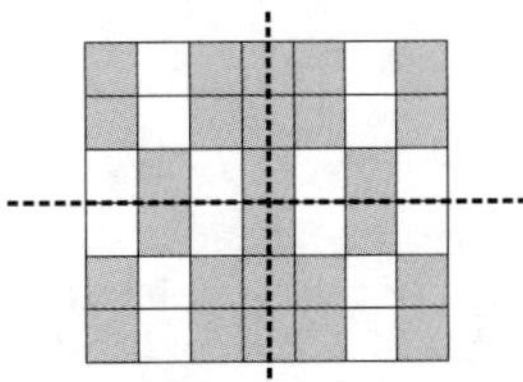

The shape has two lines of symmetry.

## 9.    60 cm
The perimeter of the fabric square is 40 cm, so each side
is 10 cm long.  So the perimeter of the blanket is
10 + 10 + 10 + 10 + 10 + 10 = 60 cm.

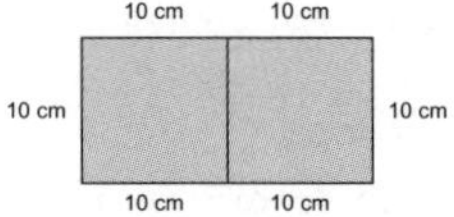


## 10.    B
A is false because 2.5 + 2 = 4.5 and 11.5 – 2 = 9.5.
C is false because 2.5 + 9 = 11.5 and 11.5 – 9 = 2.5.
D is false because 2.5 + 1 = 3.5 and 11.5 – 1 = 10.5.
E is false because 2.5 + 11.5 = 14 and 11.5 – 11.5 = 0.
B is correct because 2.5 + 4.5 = 7 and 11.5 – 4.5 = 7.

# Puzzles 5 — page 45
## Pancake Pilfering
Every minute Steve takes 3 pancakes from Rachael,
so after 3 minutes Rachael has 10 – (3 × 3) = 1 pancake.
Every minute Tracy takes 2 of Steve's pancakes,
so after 3 minutes, Tracy has 3 × 2 = 6 pancakes.
After 3 minutes, Steve has 2 + 9 – 6 = 5 pancakes.

## The Old Couples' Bus Ride
Mrs MacDonald and Mr Jones
Mrs Jones and Mr Smith
Mrs Smith and Mr Brown
Mrs Brown and Mr MacDonald

# Test 14 — pages 46-48
## 1.    35 minutes
Reading down the column, the 08:45 train arrives in Eton
at 09:20.  08:45 to 09:00 is 15 minutes.
09:00 to 09:20 is 20 minutes.
So it takes 15 + 20 = 35 minutes.

## 2.    (4, 3)
Moving 2 places right gives an $x$-coordinate of 4.
Moving 4 places down gives a $y$-coordinate of 3.
So the coordinates of point Q are (4, 3).

## 3.    C
40 is 5 times more than 8, so he needs 5 times
as much cheese for 40 people.  250 × 5 = 1250 g.

## 4.    9
A triangular prism has 9 edges.

## 5.    A
There are 6 equal sections.
3 sections are shaded, which as a fraction is $^3/_6 = ^1/_2$.

## 6.    B
24 is half of 48, so halve the answer on the right-hand
side to get the correct answer.  68 064 ÷ 2 = 34 032.

## 7.    B
A is false as the temperature
was only below 0 °C on two nights.
C is false as the most common temperature was 0 °C.
D is false as the temperature was above 3 °C on two
different nights.
B is correct because the difference
between 7 and –4 is 11, which means E is false.

## 8.    16 cm²
The next square in the sequence has sides 1 cm longer
than the previous square.  Square 4 will have
sides 4 cm long, so the area will be 4 × 4 = 16 cm².

## 9.    E
Use column addition (or partitioning) to
add all three volumes together:

```
   3 5 2
   2 3 0
 + 1 0 3
 -------
   6 8 5
```

## 10.    A
Do £16.95 + £8.65 = £25.60 (use partitioning here).
60p rounds up to the nearest pound, so in total she
spends £26 to the nearest pound.

# Test 15 — pages 49-51
## 1.    A and C
A and C are rotations of each other.

## 2.    14
The largest prime number below 10 is 7 and 7 × 2 = 14.

## 3.    3 hours, 30 minutes
Midnight is 00:00 = 24:00.  20:30 to 21:00 is
30 minutes.  21:00 to 24:00 is 3 hours.
So her alarm will go off in 3 hours, 30 minutes.

## 4.    D
Litres (l) are too big to measure the volume of a cup
sensibly, which rules out options B and E.
1 l = 1000 ml, so 25 000 ml = 25 l, so option C
is also too big.  2.5 ml is less than the amount a teaspoon
can hold, which rules out option A.
So the most sensible estimate is 250 ml.

## 5.    2
There are 14 boys in total.
12 are right-handed, so 2 boys must be left-handed.

## 6.    £11
$h$ = 6.  So Peter's phone bill costs
$h$ + 5 = 6 + 5 = £11.

## 7.    A
$^1/_4$ of 24 = 24 ÷ 4 = 6.  Dominic has read 6 books,
so he has 24 – 6 = 18 books left to read.
20% of 10 = 10 ÷ 5 = 2.  He has read 2 magazines,
so he has 10 – 2 = 8 magazines left to read.

   

**8.    D**
A is false because $^1/_4 = 0.25$.
B is false because $^1/_3 = 0.33$, and $0.33 < 0.5$.
C is false because $^7/_{10} = 0.7$.
E is false because $0.3 = ^3/_{10}$.

**9.    D**
D is the correct option because the 'Walk' sector is larger
for Class 5B than Class 5A.

**10.   15**
1 kg = 1000 g, so 6 kg = 6000 g.
So, calculate 6000 ÷ 400.  Divide both terms by 100
to get an easier division:  60 ÷ 4 = 15.

## Puzzles 6 — page 52

### Pipe Swap
Swap shaded pipe 24 with white pipe 27.

### The Wag Swag Bag Snag
The bowl (0.8 kg), picture frame (100 g = 0.1 kg)
and the dog treats (0.15 kg) is the heaviest
combination that won't tear the bag.
0.8 kg + 0.1 kg + 0.15 kg = 1.05 kg.

## Test 16 — pages 53-55

**1.    (6, 1)**
Point A is 6 squares along the $x$-axis,
and 1 square up the $y$-axis, so has coordinates of (6, 1).

**2.    4**
An obtuse angle is bigger than 90°.
There are three obtuse angles in the first shape
and one in the second shape.  3 + 1 = 4.

**3.    C**
Partition 75 into 70 + 5 and multiply 20 by each of
these parts:  70 × 20 = 1400 g,
5 × 20 = 100 g, 1400 + 100 = 1500 g.
1000 g = 1 kg, so 1500 g = 1.5 kg.

**4.    8**
Adding the previous two terms gives 3 + 5 = 8.

**5.    D**
£4.95 rounds up to £5.00.
80 × £5.00 = £400.

**6.    18**
$^1/_{10}$ of 20 = 20 ÷ 10 = 2 people.  2 people didn't go to
the party, which means 20 − 2 = 18 did go to the party.

**7.    9**
The factors of 36 are 1, 2, 3, 4, 6, 9, 12, 18, 36.
So 9 is the missing factor.

**8.    18**
The black and grey sectors of the pie chart make up
half of all the pebbles Libby found, which is 36.
So she finds 36 brown or white pebbles.
Half of these 36 are brown, so 36 ÷ 2 = 18.

**9.    20**
Find Conor's number by starting with 44 and
dividing it by 2, giving 44 ÷ 2 = 22.
Then take away 2, giving 22 − 2 = 20.

**10.   D**
If Leigh eats a sweet, there will be 10 − 1 = 9 sweets left
in the bag in total.  If she eats a red sweet,
there will be 7 − 1 = 6 red sweets left in the bag.
So $^6/_9 = ^2/_3$ sweets will be red.

## Test 17 — pages 56-58

**1.    C**
A pentagon has five straight sides.
C is the only option that has five sides.

**2.    C**
The Number Cruncher divides the numbers that go in
by 100 to get the numbers that come out.
So 7519 ÷ 100 = 75.19.

**3.    C**
Option C is false because rectangles only have two lines
of symmetry, unless they are square.

**4.    9**
From the bar chart, 12 people downloaded Talat's album
in May and 3 people downloaded his album in March.
So the difference is 12 − 3 = 9 albums.

**5.    £9**
1 kg = 1000 g, so 3 kg = 3000 g of strawberries.
So this is 3000 g ÷ 500 g = 6 bags of strawberries.
So Ana will make 6 × £1.50 = £9.

**6.    8:20 am**
Caitlin's watch shows the time as 7:55 am.
It is 25 minutes behind, so add 25 minutes to 7:55 am.
Split the 25 minutes into 5 minutes and 20 minutes.
7:55 am + 5 minutes = 8:00 am.
8:00 am + 20 minutes = 8:20 am.

**7.    E**
A gives 100 ÷ 4 = 25. B gives $^1/_{10}$ of 100
= 100 ÷ 10 = 10. C gives 10 × 2 = 20.
D gives 10% of 200 = 200 ÷ 10 = 20.
E gives 0.5 × 100 = 50. So, option E is the largest.

**8.    12 m**
The two squares together make a 4 m × 2 m rectangle.

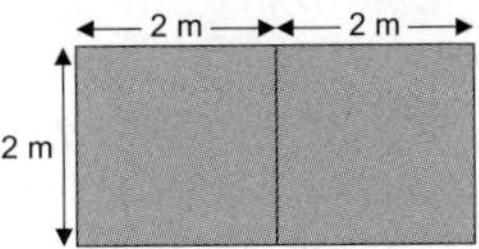


So the perimeter will be 4 + 4 + 2 + 2 = 12 m.

**9.    18.6**
To get the next term in the sequence, subtract 0.4.
19.0 − 0.4 = 18.6.

## 10.    £1.50
2 roses cost 2 × £1.20 = £2.40.  1 tulip costs £1.10.
In total, these cost £2.40 + £1.10 = £3.50.
So Astrid gets £5 − £3.50 = £1.50 change.

## Test 18 — pages 59-61
### 1.    9400 m
To round 9392 m to the nearest hundred metres, round
the digit in the hundreds column.  3 is being rounded and
9 is greater than 5, so 9392 m rounds up to 9400 m.

### 2.    300 ml
1 litre = 1000 ml, so 1.8 litres = 1800 ml.
1800 − 1500 = 300 ml,
so Tim needs 300 ml more paint.

### 3.    D
A and C are false because the area of Rosa's pond
takes up more area than one square = 1 $m^2$.
B and E are false because the area of her pond is
less than four whole squares = 4 $m^2$.

### 4.    8:05 pm
To find the time the film finishes, add 2 hours
and 45 minutes onto 5:20 pm.
5:20 pm + 2 hours = 7:20 pm.
Then split 45 minutes into 40 minutes and 5 minutes.
7:20 pm + 40 minutes = 8:00 pm.
8:00 pm + 5 minutes = 8:05 pm.

### 5.    11 years, 8 months
To find the difference in their ages, count on from the
youngest to the oldest llama.
The youngest is 6 months old.
6 months + 6 months = 1 year.
1 year + 11 years = 12 years.
12 years + 2 months = 12 years and 2 months.
So the difference in their ages is
6 months + 11 years + 2 months = 11 years, 8 months.

### 6.    30 cm
$^1/_5$ of 150 cm = 150 ÷ 5 = 30 cm.

### 7.    4
Friday has 4 symbols, and Sunday has 2 symbols.
The difference between them is 4 − 2 = 2 symbols.
Eight fewer cookies were eaten on Sunday,
so each symbol represents 8 ÷ 2 = 4 cookies.

### 8.    D
A is 0.08 away from 10.  B is 0.25 away from 10.
C is 0.5 away from 10.  D is 0.05 away from 10.
E is 0.1 away from 10.  So D is the closest to 10.

### 9.    C
The next term is found by doubling the previous term.
The next terms in the sequence are 32, 64, 128, 256,
and so on.  So 28 does not appear in the sequence.

### 10.    7 cm²
The area of the 4 cm square is 4 × 4 = 16 $cm^2$.
The area of the 3 cm square is 3 × 3 = 9 $cm^2$.
So the difference between the areas of the squares is
16 − 9 = 7 $cm^2$.

## Puzzles 7 — page 62
### Greybeard's Treasure
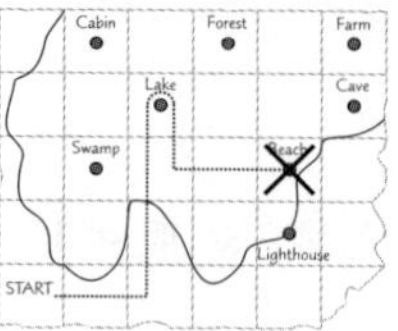


### Zoo-sual Suspects
Each animal is 1.5 m taller than the previous one,
so the next animal is 3.5 + 1.5 = 5 m tall.
Giraffe

## Test 19 — pages 63-65
### 1.    $^3/_5$
3 of the 5 squares in total are shaded, $^3/_5$.

### 2.    B
Height is a distance, so it can't be g (which measures
mass).  km and m are too big to measure the height
of a kettle sensibly and mm are too small to measure
the height of a kettle sensibly.  A kettle is usually
around 30 cm tall, so the most sensible unit is cm.

### 3.    40
10% of 400 = 400 ÷ 10 = 40 words are spelt wrong.

### 4.    4
Reading off the bar chart, 7 children said they would
prefer a rabbit and 3 children said they would prefer
a fish.  So 7 − 3 = 4 more children said they would prefer
a rabbit than a fish.

### 5.    (5, 5)
Point A is 2 squares to the left of the mirror line.
When reflected, it will be 2 squares to the right of the
mirror line.  So the new coordinates of point A are (5, 5).

### 6.    64 m²
The whole patio is a square with sides 6 + 2 = 8 m.
So the total area of the patio will be 8 × 8 = 64 $m^2$.

### 7.    E
There are five odd-numbered cards out of a total
of six cards.  As a fraction, this is $^5/_6$.

### 8.    2 weeks, 5 days
The painting takes 27 − 8 = 19 days to finish.
2 weeks = 14 days, so 19 days = 2 weeks, 5 days.

### 9.    10.5
Double Maria's skill score:  5 × 2 = 10.
Add the number in the difficulty column:  10 + 3 = 13.
Then subtract the number in the mistakes column:
13 − 2.5 = 10.5.

## 10.  C

Add the factors for each option, remembering not to include the factor that is the number itself.
A is false because its only factor is 1.
B is false because 1 + 2 = 3, which isn't 4.
C is correct because 1 + 2 + 3 = 6.
D is false because 1 + 2 + 4 = 7, which isn't 8.
E is false because 1 + 2 + 5 = 8, which isn't 10.

## Test 20 — pages 66-68

**1.  D**
1 m = 100 cm, so 30 m = 3000 cm.

**2.  −5**
Keep subtracting 6:  13 − 6 = 7.  7 − 6 = 1.
1 − 6 = −5.

**3.  3**
Round £5.95 to £6.  3 × £6 = £18 and 4 × £6 = £24, so Eimear can buy 3 teddy bears with a £20 note.

**4.  70°**
There are 180° along a straight line.
So angle $x$ = 180° − 110° = 70°.

**5.  5**
The shape has five lines of symmetry, as shown below.

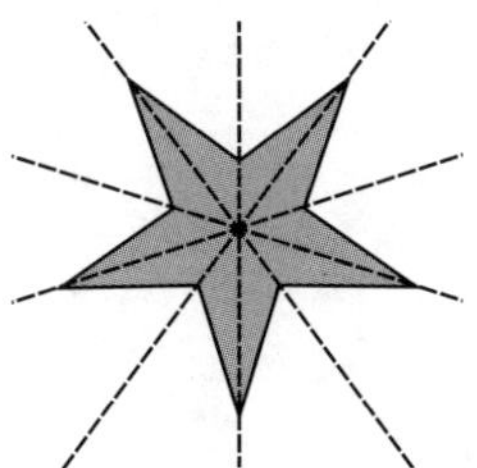

**6.  14.5 s**
The slowest swimmer was Eva with 45.9 s and the fastest swimmer was Joan with 31.4 s.  So the difference between the two is 45.9 s − 31.4 s = 14.5 s.

**7.  18:00**
The cats had slept for the same total number of hours where their lines on the graph cross.
This happened at 18:00.

**8.  2 cm**
The volume of the box = 20 cm³ = 2 × 5 × ? = 10 × ?.
So ? = 2 cm.

**9.  A**
The spinner is fair, so the sectors are the same size.
There is one sector for mist out of a total of five sectors.
As a fraction, this is $^1/_5 = {}^{20}/_{100}$ = 20%.

## 10.  324 cm

Use long multiplication to work out the tree's growth over 12 years (27 cm × 12):

```
    27
  ×  12
    54
   270
   324
```

## Puzzles 8 — page 69

**Wires Gone Haywire**
A: 6 × 4 = 24
B: 12 × 3 = 36
C: 9 × 6 = 54
D: 18 × 2 = 36
So A and C have the wrong bulb attached.

**Connie's Coin Conundrum**
The middle keyring costs 38p = 20p, 10p, 5p, 2p and 1p.
So the middle keyring is the correct option.
The other keyrings cannot be bought with exactly the right amount of money.

## Test 21 — pages 70-72

**1.  28 cm**
The square has four sides of 7 cm.
Its perimeter is 4 × 7 = 28 cm.

**2.  £4.25**
Sarah's food costs a total of £5.50 + £0.75 + £1.50 = £7.75 (use partitioning if needed).
The amount of money she has left over is £12 − £7.75.  Partition £7.75 into £7 and £0.75 and subtract these from £12.  £12 − £7 = £5, £5 − £0.75 = £4.25.  So Sarah will have £4.25 left over.

**3.  A**
Jack's shape is made up of 4 squares.
B and C are false because they are made up of 5 squares.
D is false because it is made up of 6 squares.
E is false because it is made up of 9 squares.
A is correct because it is made up of 4 squares.

**4.  3500 g**
Each litre weighs 1 kg, so 3 litres weigh 3 kg.
1 kg = 1000 g, so 3 kg = 3000 g.
So the total weight of the water and bucket is 3000 + 500 = 3500 g.

**5.  C**
Start with 10, and count back in 4s three times:
10 − 4 = 6, 6 − 4 = 2, 2 − 4 = −2.

**6.  C**
Look for the tallest and shortest bars.
The tallest bar is Friday and the shortest is Monday, so the greatest difference is between these two days.
This is option C.





Answers

**7.    E**
A is false as 487 rounded to the nearest 10 is 490.
B is false as 599 rounded to the nearest 100 is 600.
C is false as 525 rounded to the nearest 1000
is 1000.
D is false as 506 rounded to the nearest 10 is 510.
E is correct as 453 rounded to the nearest 100 is 500.

**8.    48 m³**
The volume of the cuboid is width × length × height
= 2 × 12 × 2 = 48 m³.

**9.    80°**
There are 360° around a point.  360° − 100° − 100°
= 160°.  The two missing angles $x$ are the same,
so they measure 160° ÷ 2 = 80° each.

**10.    13**
April lost $^1/_4$ of her games: $^1/_4$ of 20 = 20 ÷ 4 = 5
games.  She drew 10% of her games:
10% of 20 = 20 ÷ 10 = 2 games.
And she won the rest: 20 − 5 − 2 = 13.

# Test 22 — pages 73-75
**1.    3508**
Three thousand, five hundred and eight means 3
in the thousands column, 5 in the hundreds column,
0 in the tens column and 8 in the ones column.

**2.    45 mm**
The length of the pencil is from 0 on the centimetre ruler
to the line halfway between 4 and 5 cm, or 4.5 cm.

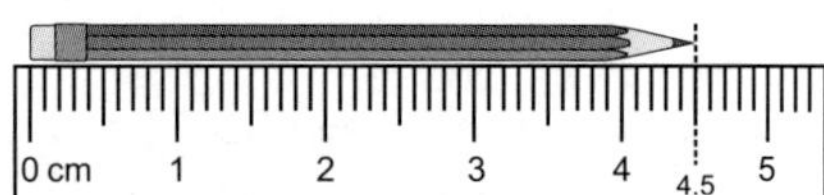

1 cm = 10 mm, so 4.5 cm = 45 mm.

**3.    5**
The left side of the equals sign is 10 + 10 + 10 = 30.
So 6 × the missing number = 30.
6 × 5 = 30, so 5 is the missing number.

**4.    B**
Point T is further away from zero than point S
on both the $x$-axis and the $y$-axis.
This means the $x$ and $y$-coordinates of point T must be
greater than the $x$ and $y$-coordinates of point S.
A, C, D and E are false because they don't have greater $x$
and $y$-coordinates than point S.

**5.    £3.60**
1 litre = 1000 ml, so 3 litres = 3000 ml.
Nathan needs 3000 ÷ 500 = 6 times as much milk.
So the milk costs 60p × 6 = 360p = £3.60.

**6.    $3**

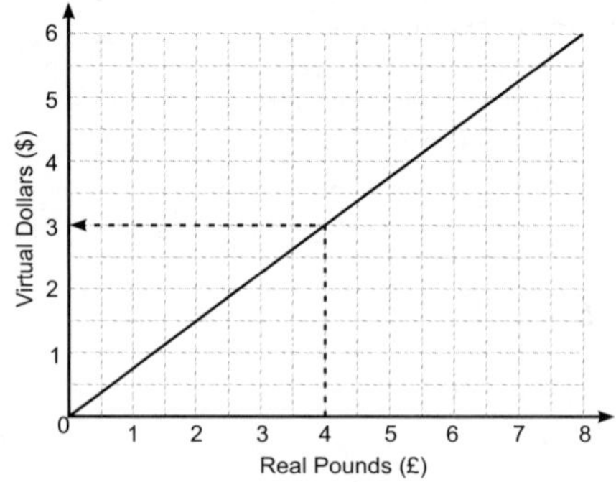


Read up from £4 and then across to the $y$-axis.
Jessica receives $3.

**7.    A**
The number of bananas is $^1/_{10}$ of 20,
which is 20 ÷ 10 = 2.  The number of mangoes is
20% of 20, which is 20 ÷ 5 = 4.
The number of oranges is 20 − 2 − 4 = 14.
So the most popular fruit in the class is oranges.

**8.    15**
Matthew's age is 33 minus Rebecca's age.  Rebecca is
3 years older, so once 3 is taken off, their ages will be the
same:  33 − 3 = 30.  30 ÷ 2 = 15, so Rebecca's age is
15 + 3 = 18 and Matthew's age is 15.

**9.    D**
Angle $x$ and angle $y$ added together form a right angle.
A right angle is 90°, so $x + y$ = 90°.

**10.    13:00**
The Manchester train arrives every 2 hours.
If the Manchester train arrives at 7:00, it will also arrive
at 9:00, 11:00, 13:00, 15:00 and 17:00.
The Birmingham train arrives every 3 hours.
If the Birmingham train arrives at 7:00, it will also arrive
at 10:00, 13:00 and 16:00.
The next time they both arrive at
Preston station is 13:00.

# Test 23 — pages 76-78
**1.    22**
Work out the brackets first.
36 − (7 × 2) = 36 − 14 = 22.

**2.    A**
5 is not a factor of 24 because you cannot divide
24 by 5 and get a whole number answer.
3 is a factor of 24 because 24 ÷ 3 = 8.
2 is a factor of 24 because 24 ÷ 2 = 12.
4 is a factor of 24 because 24 ÷ 4 = 6.
6 is a factor of 24 because 24 ÷ 6 = 4.
So the correct answer is A.

          

**3.     C**
In the butterfly house there are 6 Red Admiral,
9 Common Blue, 2 Small Heath, 3 Green Hairstreak and
10 Wood White.
So $\frac{1}{3}$ of Common Blue is $9 \div 3 = 3$.  The butterfly type
with a population of 3 is Green Hairstreak.

**4.     6**
£5 = 500p, so the amount of books Damon can buy is
$500 \div 80$.  Make this simpler by dividing both numbers by
10: $50 \div 8 = 6$ r 2, so Damon can buy 6 books.

**5.     2800 g**
The weight of Jayden's cakes is $8 \times 350\,g = 2800\,g$.

**6.     34 cm**
Find the missing lengths.

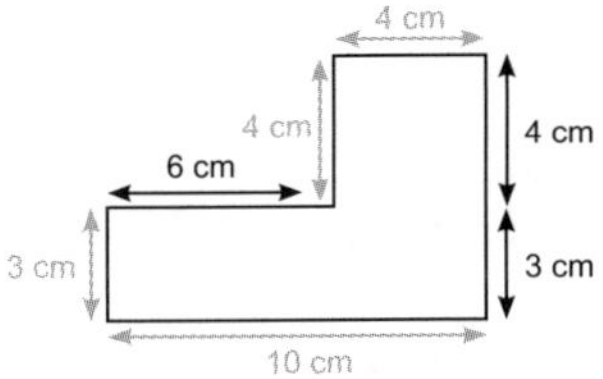

Add the length of each side together:
$3 + 6 + 4 + 4 + 4 + 3 + 10 = 34\,cm$.

**7.     D**
The smallest mug holds 200 ml.  Noam pours 25% of
$200\,ml = 200 \div 4 = 50\,ml$ out of the mug.
This means $200 - 50 = 150\,ml$ coffee is
left in the mug, which is option D.

**8.     15**
Each week Zara catches three more criminals than she
did the previous week.  So as she caught 9 criminals
in week 3, she will catch 12 criminals in week 4 and
15 criminals in week 5.

**9.     900 m²**
The car park is a 50 m × 20 m rectangle with a
10 m × 10 m square removed.
$50 \times 20 = 1000\,m^2$.  $10 \times 10 = 100\,m^2$.
So the car park has an area of $1000 - 100 = 900\,m^2$.

**10.     £120**
1 patio slab costs $£20 \div 5 = £4$.
So 30 patio slabs will cost $30 \times £4 = £120$.

# Puzzles 9 — page 79
## Sheep Separation
Each group adds up to 9.

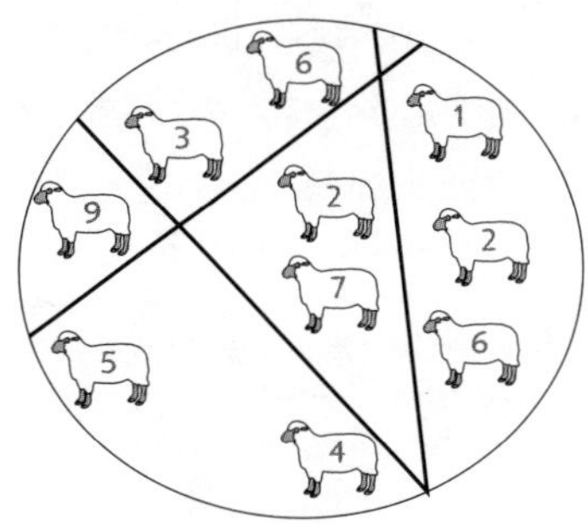

## Shape Selection
Lucy:  A, Martin:  D, Nathan:  C, Olivia:  B.

# Test 24 — pages 80-82
**1.     B**
If Caspar is facing North and then turns
90° anticlockwise he will be facing West.

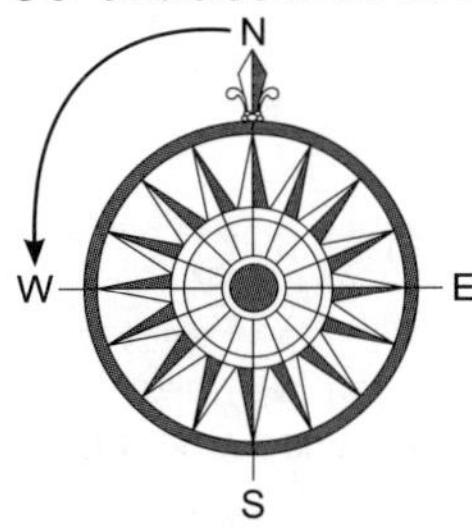


**2.     E**
Options A, B, C and D are all suitable units of
measurement.  E is false because the distance between
the Earth and the Moon is very large and millimetres
are best used to measure very small distances.

**3.     D**
On Monday Arthur made $500 + 200 = 700$ pins.
On Tuesday Arthur made $300 + 400 = 700$ pins.
On Wednesday Arthur made $200 + 600 = 800$ pins.
On Thursday Arthur made $400 + 500 = 900$ pins.
On Friday Arthur made $700 + 100 = 800$ pins.
So Arthur made the most pins on Thursday.

**4.     £0.60**
Take away the cost of one whole loaf from £3:
$£3 - £1.20 = £1.80$.
She buys three half loaves for £1.80:
$£1.80 \div 3 = £0.60$.

**5.    21%**
Easter takes up the space between 55% and 76% on the chart.

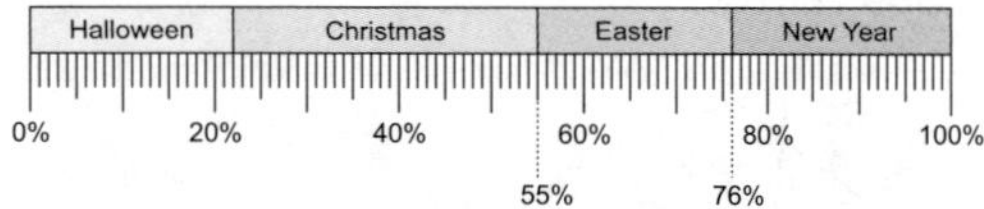

So the percentage of the class who said Easter was 76% – 55% = 21%.

**6.    16**
To find Ebony's original number, work backwards through her method. First take away 4: 52 – 4 = 48. Then divide by 3: 48 ÷ 3 = 16. So Ebony's original number was 16.

**7.    (5, 4)**
To find the coordinates of point R, find the coordinates of the point halfway between point P and point Q.

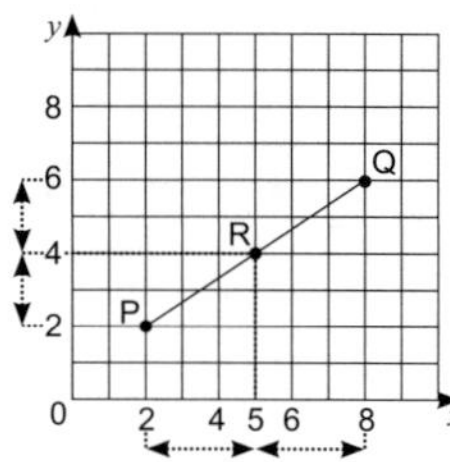

So the coordinates of point R are (5, 4).

**8.    C**
A is false because it is a rotated reflection of shape S. B, D and E are false because they are not the same shape as shape S.

**9.    Offer A**
25% of 200 is 200 ÷ 4 = 50.
So offer A costs £200 – £50 = £150.
Offer B costs £200 – £60 = £140, plus £10.50, so offer B costs £140 + £10.50 = £150.50.
So offer A is the cheapest.

**10.    8**
There are 10 red candles.
To find $\frac{2}{5}$ of 10, do 10 ÷ 5 = 2, then 2 × 2 = 4.
There are 8 blue candles. $\frac{1}{2}$ of 8 = 8 ÷ 2 = 4.
So the total number of candles Jaya lights is 4 + 4 = 8.

# Test 25 — pages 83-85

**1.    B**
A is false as 65 rounded to the nearest 10 is 70.
B is correct as 55 rounded to the nearest 10 is 60.
C is false as 67 rounded to the nearest 10 is 70.
D is false as 95 rounded to the nearest 10 is 100.
E is false as 70 rounded to the nearest 10 is 70.

**2.    D**
The shape has four sides, with two sets of parallel sides and no right angles, so it is a parallelogram.

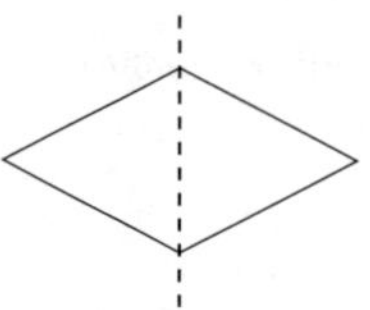

**3.    £13.50**
Bart pays with £10 + £10 = £20.
He spends £20 – £6.50.
Partition £6.50 into £6 + £0.50 and subtract each.
£20 – £6 = £14, £14 – £0.50 = £13.50.
So the stationery cost £13.50.

**4.    6**
32 × 3 = 96. So Gabriella wants to plant 3 times as many daffodils this year as last year.
So she will need 3 × 2 = 6 bags of soil.

**5.    C**
A is false because 1 × 2 + 1 = 3, which isn't the second term in the sequence. B is false because 2 × 2 + 1 = 5, which isn't the second term in the sequence. D is false because 3 × 2 + 1 = 7, which isn't the second term in the sequence. E is false because 3 × 2 + 1 = 7, which isn't the second term in the sequence.

**6.    E**
Joel arrives at 16:05. The film started 10 minutes before this, at 15:55. The film will finish 2 hours after 15:55 at 17:55, which is option E.

**7.    $\frac{5}{11}$**
The total number of stamps is 5 + 4 + 2 = 11. There are 5 red stamps, so the fraction of red stamps is $\frac{5}{11}$.

**8.    135 cm**
50% of 90 cm = 90 ÷ 2 = 45 cm.
So Jane's height is 90 + 45 = 135 cm.

**9.    D**
The values on the profit axis go up unevenly. The values go up in 20s, then 5s, then 2s. This means it is difficult to see how much the profit has changed over the years.

**10.    30 cm**
The diagram shows a square, so each side of the square is 6 cm. This means the base of the equilateral triangle is 6 cm, so the other sides of the triangle are also 6 cm. There are five sides on the shape, so the perimeter is 5 × 6 = 30 cm.

# Puzzles 10 — page 86

## Number Web

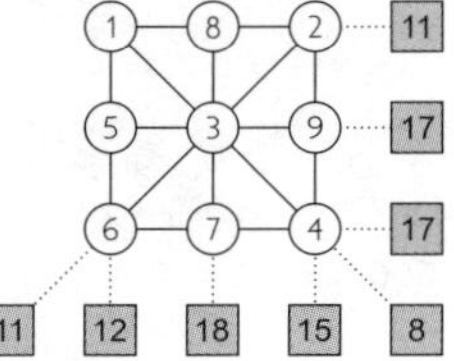

## The Suit Pursuit

He was at the bank for 40 minutes.
40 minutes before 2:30 is 1:50.
He left the shop 3 hours before this.
3 hours before 1:50 is 10:50.
The suit was stolen 30 minutes before this.
30 minutes before 10:50 is 10:20.

# Test 26 — pages 87-89

**1.    B**
The digit is two places to the left of the decimal point.
This is the tens column.

**2.    C**
Depth is a distance, so it can't be ml (which measures
volume) or kg (which measures mass).  Both mm and cm
are too small to measure the depth of the deepest part
of the ocean sensibly.  So the most sensible unit is km.

**3.    7.8 m**
The longest throw is 780 cm.
1 m = 100 cm, so 780 cm = 7.8 m.

**4.    (4, 4)**
Moving three squares to the right gives an $x$-coordinate
of 1 + 3 = 4.  Moving two squares up gives a $y$-coordinate
of 2 + 2 = 4.  The new coordinates of point X are (4, 4).

**5.    C**

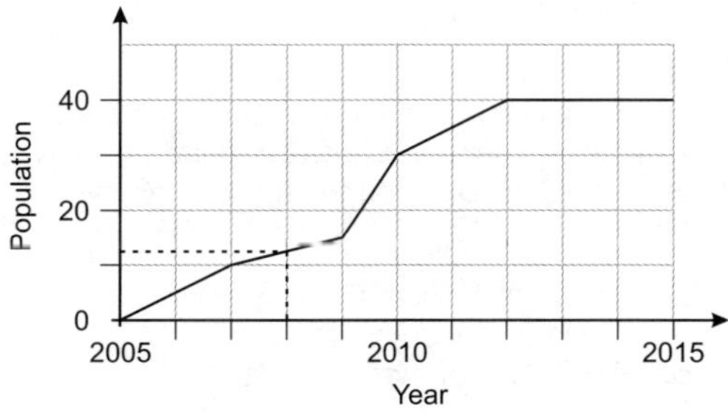

The estimated population is more than 10, so options
A and D are ruled out.  The estimated population is
less than 20, so option E is ruled out.  The estimated
population is nearer 10 than 20, so option B is ruled out.

**6.    4**
There are three dots on the top of the dice, so 7 − 3 = 4.
So there will be 4 dots on the bottom of the dice.

**7.    4**
There are three numbers, so 8 × 2 × ? = 64.
Divide 64 by 2 and then by 8 to get the missing number.
64 ÷ 2 = 32, 32 ÷ 8 = 4.  So the third number Anisha
thinks of is 4.

**8.    E**
16 has a factor of 2 and a factor of 4, so option A is
ruled out.  12 has a factor of 3 and a factor of 4,
so option B is ruled out.  36 has a factor of 3 and a
factor of 4, so option C is ruled out.  20 has a
factor of 2 and a factor of 5, so option D is ruled out.

**9.    60%**
After Terry has given 20 pennies to his sister, he has
50 − 20 = 30 left.  Dividing 30 into three piles,
gives 30 ÷ 3 = 10 in each pile.  So his sister will have
20 + 10 = 30 pennies.  $^{30}/_{50} = {}^{60}/_{100}$ = 60%.
So Terry's sister will have 60% of his original 50 pennies.

**10.    12 cm³**
The length of the missing side on the white part of the
rubber is 5 − 2 = 3 cm.  So the volume of the white part
of the rubber is 2 × 2 × 3 = 12 cm³.

# Test 27 — pages 90-92

**1.    $^2/_9$**
2 of the 9 squares are shaded, so $^2/_9$ of the grid
has been shaded.

**2.    1997**
If Cerys was born in 2004, Jenna was born in
2004 − 5 = 1999.  So Shireen was born in
1999 − 2 = 1997.

**3.    17**
14 can be divided by 2, so isn't a prime number.
15 can be divided by 3, so isn't a prime number.
16 can be divided by 2, so isn't a prime number.
So the next prime number after 13 is 17.

**4.    B**
Turning 90° anticlockwise means turning one right angle
to the left.  If Nora was facing south, she'd be facing east
after turning.

**5.    E**
A is false because the total number of spots on
all three ladybirds is 19, which is less than 20.
B is false because 19 is not a multiple of 3.
C is false because 19 is not an even number.
D is false because 19 is not a square number.

**6.    C**
The new point P will be the same distance from the
mirror line as the old point P was.  It is now at (6, 3).

**7.    D**
$^1/_4$ of adults cannot drive.  $^1/_4$ of 60 is 60 ÷ 4 = 15.





Answers

**8.    12 m**
Double the lengths of the smaller triangle.
$2.5 \times 2 = 5$ m, $1.5 \times 2 = 3$ m and $2 \times 2 = 4$ m.
So the perimeter of the bigger triangle is
$5 + 3 + 4 = 12$ m.

**9.    1200 ml**
1 litre = 1000 ml, so 0.1 litres = 100 ml.
So $100 \times 12 = 1200$ ml water will have been
poured into the basin.

**10.    B**
The volume of a cube is length × width × height.
The length, width and height of the cube are all $x$,
so the correct expression is $x \times x \times x$, which is option B.

# Test 28 — pages 93-95
**1.    C**
Multiplying the top and bottom numbers of
the fraction by 5 gives $^5/_{15}$.

**2.    £2.75**
A prawn cocktail costs £2.50 and steak & chips costs
£4.75, so the total cost = £2.50 + £4.75.
Partition £4.75 into £4 + £0.75 and add
each part separately:  £2.50 + £4 = £6.50,
£6.50 + £0.75 = £7.25.
So the cost of ice cream is £10 – £7.25.
£10 – £7 = £3, £3 – £0.25 = £2.75.

**3.    B**
A is false because $1 + 2 + 3 = 6$, which is not a square
number. B is correct because $2 + 3 + 4 = 9 = 3^2$.
C is false because $3 + 4 + 5 = 12$, which is not a square
number. D is false because $4 + 5 + 6 = 15$, which is not a
square number. E is false because $5 + 6 + 7 = 18$,
which is not a square number.

**4.    3000**
Partition 12 into 10 + 2 and multiply each part
separately: $250 \times 10 = 2500$, $250 \times 2 = 500$,
$2500 + 500 = 3000$.

**5.    50%**
Song W is 10 minutes long, song X is 3 minutes long,
song Y is 6 minutes long and song Z is 9 minutes long.
2 out of four songs are less than 8 minutes long.
This is $^2/_4$, or $^1/_2 = 50\%$.

**6.    14:05**
The clock currently shows the time as being 15:25.
Take away 1 hour and 20 minutes:
15:25 – 1 hour = 14:25, 14:25 – 20 minutes = 14:05.

**7.    37.3 cm**
In 3 weeks, the sunflower would grow $2.3 \times 3 = 6.9$ cm.
So at the end of 3 weeks the sunflower will be
$30.4 + 6.9 = 37.3$ cm tall.

**8.    12 m²**
Each rectangle has an area of $1 \times 3 = 3$ m².
The flag is made of four rectangles,
so the area is $4 \times 3 = 12$ m².

**9.    D**
50% of Sasha's scarves are blue and 30% are grey.
So 100% – 50% – 30% = 20% are white.
$20\% = ^{20}/_{100} = ^1/_5$.

**10.    E**
A is correct because $3 \times 4 = 12$. B is correct because
$4 + 3 = 7$. C is correct because $3 + 4 = 7$. D is correct
because $4 + 4 = 8$. E is not correct because $3 – 4 = –1$.

# Puzzles 11 — page 96
**The Knight's Tour**
A: 2, B: 4, C: 3, D: 2

# Test 29 — pages 97-99
**1.    D**
Angle $y$ is smaller than a right angle so options A and E
are ruled out.  Angle $y$ is greater than half a right angle
(45°) so options B and C are ruled out.

**2.    600 g**
$36 = 12 \times 3$, so she needs 3 times as much flour for
36 brownies.  $200 \times 3 = 600$ g.

**3.    B**
$^1/_2$ of a wheel icon represents $4 \div 2 = 2$ cars,
and $^1/_4$ of a wheel icon represents $4 \div 4 = 1$ car.
A is false as there are $8 + 2 + 7 + 1 = 18$ cars in total.
B is correct as there are 2 black cars, and $4 \times 2 = 8$,
which is the number of the blue cars.
C is false as blue has the most wheel icons.
D is false as white has the least wheel icons.
E is false as red has $1^3/_4$ wheel icons = $4 + 3 = 7$,
and white has $^1/_4$ of a wheel icon = 1.
So the difference between them is $7 – 1 = 6$.

**4.    19**
Each term is found by adding 3 to the previous term.
The sixth term in the sequence is $13 + 3 = 16$,
and the seventh term is $16 + 3 = 19$.

**5.    296 ml**
$63.2 + 232.4 = 295.6$ ml (use partitioning if needed).
To the nearest millilitre, the 5 needs to be rounded.
6 is bigger than 5, so 295.6 ml rounds up to 296 ml.

**6.    39 m²**
The whole rectangle has an area of $6 \times 8 = 48$ m².
The square has an area of $3 \times 3 = 9$ m².
So she has $48 – 9 = 39$ m² of material left.

**7.    4**
Each chair costs £24.  Two chairs cost
£24 + £24 = £48, three chairs cost
£48 + £24 = £72, four chairs cost £72 + £24 = £96,
five chairs cost £96 + £24 = £120.  Elisa has £110,
so she can get 4 chairs but doesn't have enough money
for 5.

**8.    C**
January had 10 mm and March had 30 mm of rainfall.
Because the rainfall increased by the same amount each
month, February must be halfway between 10 mm and
30 mm, which is 20 mm.  The rainfall increases by 10 mm
each month, so April would have 30 + 10 = 40 mm of
rainfall, which is option C.

**9.    8**
6 of the fish are koi, and this is $^3/_8$ of the total number
of fish.  This means that $^1/_8$ of the total number of fish in
the pond is 6 ÷ 3 = 2 fish.  $^1/_2$ = $^4/_8$, so there must be
4 × 2 = 8 goldfish in the pond.

**10.   80%**
She doesn't camp for 8 days out of a total of 10 days.
As a fraction, this is $^8/_{10}$ = $^{80}/_{100}$ = 80%.

# Test 30 — pages 100-102
**1.    B**
Look at the place value for each digit from right to left.
There are 8 ones, which rules out option D.
There are 0 tens, which rules out options A and E.
There are 3 thousands, which rules out option C.

**2.    E**
From above you can see 4 cubes, which rules out
options B, C and D.  There is 1 cube at the bottom,
which rules out option A.

**3.    9 mm**
6 × ? = 54 mm$^2$.  6 × 9 = 54,
so the length of the missing side is 9 mm.

**4.    44%**
She has 50 – 28 = 22 action films
out of a total of 50 DVDs.
This as a fraction is $^{22}/_{50}$.  $^{22}/_{50}$ = $^{44}/_{100}$ = 44%.

**5.    A**
Option B is false because a square-based pyramid has
1 square face.  Option C is false because
a triangular prism has 3 rectangular faces.
Option D is false because a cone has 1 circular face.
Option E is false because a cuboid has
6 rectangular faces.

**6.    B**
The factors of 15 are 1, 3, 5 and 15.
The factors of 27 are 1, 3, 9 and 27.
The only common factor in the given options is 3.

**7.    –8**
Each term is found by taking away 3 from the
previous term.  So the fifth term is –5 – 3 = –8.

**8.    24**
Arianna has 2 times as many stickers as Francis.
Share 36 into 3 equal parts and give 1 part to Francis,
and 2 parts to Arianna.  36 ÷ 3 = 12.
12 + 12 = 24, so Francis has 12 stickers
and Arianna has 24.

**9.    B**
There are 360° around a point.  75° + 82° = 157°.
So angle $x$ = 360° – 157° = 203°.

**10.   280 000 cm**
1 km = 1000 m, so 2.8 km = 2800 m.
1 m = 100 cm, so 2800 m = 280 000 cm.

# Test 31— pages 103-105
**1.    11.2 cm**
There are 10 divisions between 11 cm and 12 cm, so
each division is worth 1 ÷ 10 = 0.1 cm.
The arrow is pointing to 2 divisions after 11 cm, so it is
pointing to 11.2 cm.

**2.    40%**
There are 6 short-haired guinea pigs and 10 guinea pigs
altogether, so there must be 4 that are long-haired.
4 out of 10 as a fraction is $^4/_{10}$.
$^4/_{10}$ = $^{40}/_{100}$ = 40%.

**3.    D**
1 week = 7 days, so 3 weeks = 3 × 7 days = 21 days.
21 days after the 4th May would be the 25th May.

**4.    8**
$4^2$ = 4 × 4 = 16.  Lubo has half of 16 which is 16 ÷ 2 = 8.

**5.    (7, 6)**
The bottom-right point has coordinates (7, 2).
The final point will have the same $x$-coordinate (7).
The top-left point has coordinates (2, 6).
The final point will have the same $y$-coordinate (6).
So the coordinates of the final point are (7, 6).

**6.    D**
680 = 340 + 340 = 340 × 2.  680 is added
four times, which is the same as adding
340 eight times = 340 × 8.

**7.    A**
Option B gives 10% of £10 000
= £10 000 ÷ 10 = £1000.
Option C gives $^1/_{20}$ of £10 000
= £10 000 ÷ 20 = £500.
Option D gives £100 000 ÷ 100 = £1000.
Option E gives (£5 + £5) × 100 = £10 × 100
= £1000.
£1500 is the largest, so option A is the correct answer.

**8.    5 °C**
Read off the graph:

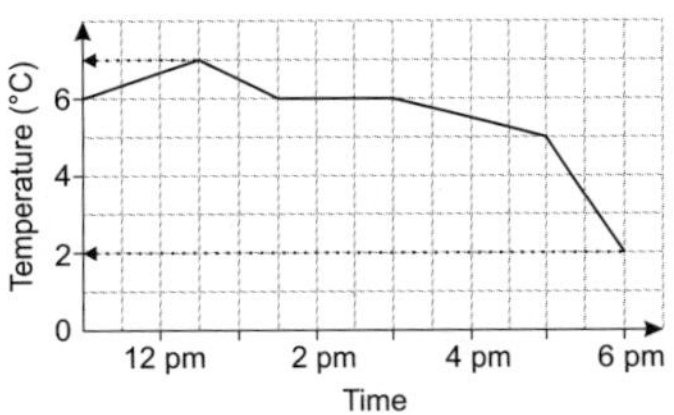


The highest temperature is 7 °C and the lowest is 2 °C.
So the difference between them is 7 – 2 = 5 °C.

     123     Answers

**9.   E**

There are 12 tourists and 36 people altogether,
so there are 36 − 12 = 24 who aren't tourists.
24 out of 36 people as a fraction is $^{24}/_{36}$.
Simplify $^{24}/_{36}$ by dividing by 12 = $^{2}/_{3}$, which is option E.

**10.   12**

32 − 8 = 24. ★ × 2 = 24, so ★ = 12.

## Puzzles 12 — page 106

### Captain Codebreaker's Calamity

YOU WILL NEVER CATCH ME.
YOU CRACKED THE CODE.  HOORAY!

Cloud:  3 + 12 + 15 + 21 + 4 = 55
Fox:  6 + 15 + 24 = 45
Rocket:  18 + 15 + 3 + 11 + 5 + 20 = 72







M5XPE2